MW01040999

A School-Wide Approach to Student-Led Conferences

A Practitioner's Guide

by

Patti Kinney

Mary Beth Munroe

Pam Sessions

National Middle School Association
Westerville, Ohio

National Middle School Association
4151 Executive Parkway
Suite 300
Westerville, Ohio 43081
Telephone (800) 528-NMSA

Copyright ©2000 by National Middle School Association.

All rights reserved. No part of this publication may be reproduced or transmitted in any form or by any means, electronic or mechanical, without permission in writing from the publisher except in the case of brief quotations embodied in reviews or articles. The materials presented herein are the expressions of the authors and do not necessarily represent the policies of NMSA. NMSA is a registered servicemark of National Middle School Association.

Printed in the United States of America.

Sue Swaim, Executive Director
Jeff Ward, Associate Executive Director
John Lounsbury, Senior Editor, Professional Publications
Edward Brazee, Associate Editor, Professional Publications
Mary Mitchell, Copy Editor/Designer
Marcia Meade, Senior Publications Representative

Library of Congress Cataloging-in-Publication Data
Kinney, Patti, date
   A school-wide approach to student-led conferences: a practitioner's guide/by Patti Kinney, Mary Beth Munroe, Pam Sessions.
      p. cm.
   Includes bibliographical references (p.).
   ISBN 1-56090-164-0
   1. Student-led parent conferences. 2. Portfolios in education. I. Munroe, Mary Beth, date- II. Sessions, Pam, date- III. Title.

LC225.5 .K56 2000
371.103--dc21

                                                      00-030456

Contents

Dedicated to the remarkable students, staff, and parents of
Talent Middle School,
Talent, Oregon.

Foreword

Occasionally you come across a program, method, or activity that really makes so much sense that you wonder, "Why didn't I think of this a long time ago?" The concept of student-led conferences is such an idea.

While teaching in Colorado, I stumbled on student-led conferences largely by accident. Over lunch at a middle school conference one day I happened to talk to teachers who were exploring the idea of their students' preparing and presenting information at the next set of parent conferences. I was immediately intrigued. However, it was not until my colleague, Ginny Ramage, and her teammates decided to implement student-led conferences at our school, Scott Carpenter Middle School, that I began to seriously explore this awesome approach to conferences.

Several aspects of student-led conferences appeal to me. First, the teacher has a very different role in the conference. No longer the focal point of others' discussion, the student now runs the conference. Questions, concerns, and responses come directly from the student. The teacher facilitates, listens in on the conference, and offers assistance when needed.

After exploring the validity of student-led conferences it was time to discuss the idea with my team. At first, there was apprehension and concern about the process. Two issues surfaced: How to inform our students' parents about this new process? And would they accept the idea that teachers would not lead the conference? The second issue was how would our students handle this approach? Would they be able to conduct effective conferences with their parents?

After we talked ourselves off the ledge of doubt and frustration, we sat down as a team and began to answer some of our questions. We discovered that this type of conference allowed students to assume ownership of their education. For us, that was really all the incentive we needed. Like most teams, we had a tendency to take on more than we could handle. When this happens frustration sets in and we lose our focus of what is right and best for our students. Instituting student-led conferences also allowed us to move the center of responsibility to the students – where it should be – and bring students and their families together to talk about the educational progress of students.

This new resource, *A School-Wide Approach to Student-Led Conferences,* delivers on its promise. It is a practitioner's guide, taking the reader through each step of the process. From answering the questions my team raised, to selecting work that students would include, describing the new roles of students and teachers, preparing for the conference, and finally suggesting ways to assess the whole process, this book is a gold mine for any teacher, team, or school interested in moving toward student-led conferences.

Bringing families together to talk about learning, progress, and future needs is paramount to this process. Parents, teachers, and students need to work together to discuss academic success, personal goals, homework, social issues, and personal struggles with their young adolescents during this critical period of development. In traditional parent-teacher conferences, the most important person – the student – is left out. With student-led conferences, no longer will the teacher have to answer questions that the student should answer. For example, in a parent-teacher conference a teacher might be asked by a parent why a son or daughter is not doing homework. Why should the teacher answer this question? Certainly young adolescents are capable of taking more responsibility for their learning, and student-led conferences offers them both opportunities and challenges for doing so.

One aspect critical to the success of student-led conferences is planning and preparation. And that is why this book is so valuable. It provides realistic ideas on how to organize yourself and your team. It also offers practical advice and reproducible letters for parents. Simply put, it is the mini-mart of student-led conferences; you can do all of your shopping from this book. So pick it up, spend some time reading it, and then get started.

Jack C. Berckemeyer
Director of Member and Affiliate Services,
National Middle School Association,
and former sixth grade teacher

1.

Setting the Stage

I t's parent-teacher conference time, and there's a sense of urgency in the air. Hurried conversations occur across tables. While parents stand around impatiently glancing at their watches and waiting their turn, the sound of chimes breaks into the hum of voices. Conversations are quickly cut off as people shuffle from one place to another. Another round of conferences has begun. Teachers are available, sitting at tables packed together in the commons area. Looking around the crowded room it is apparent that some teachers will face a never-ending stream of parents while others sit idly for long periods of time. And, despite the fact that conversations revolve around the progress of middle school students, there's a curious lack of middle school students present.

Sound familiar? Had you attended conference time at our school in past years, you would have observed this scene hour after hour, day after day. Today, things are different. Since our move to student-led conferences several years ago the pace has slowed despite the fact that parent attendance has jumped from forty-five percent to nearly ninety-five percent. Imagine the following scenario at your school.

Students and parents enter the school together, are welcomed at the front door and offered directions and refreshments. They arrive at the conference room, and after a brief introduction to the conference facilitator the conference begins with students reading a letter written to their parent or guardian.

Dear Mother and Father,

Thank you for coming to my student-led conference. I have worked on many projects this trimester and have done my work with better organization. My favorite piece of work is my coffee-stained book cover. I like it because I spent a lot of time and put a lot of hard work into it. My next favorite is band because I'm doing a good job on the French horn.

Again, I'm glad you came to my conference. I hope it lets you see all of the things I do in school (only the good things I hope).

At the end of this conference I have two goals written. It would be nice if you would write a third one with me.

Sincerely,
Tim

Students and parents enter the school together, are welcomed at the front door, and offered directions and refreshments.

As the conference continues, the student leads his/her parents through a prepared portfolio of work, sharing and discussing the skills, processes, and content learned by doing each piece. The conference ends with the student and parents setting goals for the coming school year. For most of the time the conference facilitator remained in the background, stepping in only when needed.

Student-led conferences began at Talent Middle School (TMS) about seven years ago with two teachers using the process with their language arts-social studies classes. As they shared the results with the staff, interest and excitement grew, and more teachers joined in each year until 1996, when we devised a plan where all students and teachers participated in the process. This book tells our story, describes our plan, and is designed to help you make student-led conferences a reality at your school. But first, let's look at why this shift in conferencing procedures was necessary.

Those of us who work in middle schools know that early adolescence is a trying time for young people (and the adults around them) as they struggle with issues of identity and independence. In designing effective assessment procedures, it is critical to take these developmental needs into account. *This We Believe* (1995), NMSA's position paper for developmentally responsive middle level schools, states

> *Since early adolescence is a crucial period in establishing a clear self-concept and positive self-esteem, assessment and evaluation should emphasize individual progress rather than comparison with other students. The goal is to help students discover and understand their strengths, weaknesses, interests, values, and personalities. Student self-evaluation is an important means of developing a fair and realistic self-concept.* (p. 27)

While the purpose of the traditional parent-teacher conference is admirable, it does not meet these developmental standards and generally has little long-term impact on academic improvement. It is ironic that a primary purpose of parent-teacher conferences has been to encourage students to accept more responsibility for their learning and their actions, yet students have rarely been involved in the process. Instead of being invited to participate in discussions regarding their academic achievement, students were left at home to wonder what was being said behind their backs or to worry about which of their misdeeds their teachers would tell their parents. Student-led conferences shift the focus back to where it belongs – the student.

In our experience, the benefits of student-led conferences far outweigh the considerable effort needed to create a successful school-wide experience for the students. Student accountability is the key. Richard Stiggins (1999) believes that the student-led conference process

> *...is the biggest breakthrough in communicating about student achievement in the last century. When students are well prepared over an extended period to tell the story of their own success (or lack thereof), they seem to experience a fundamental shift in their internal sense of responsibility for that success. The pride in accomplishment that students feel when they have a positive story to tell and tell it well can be immensely motivational. The sense of personal responsibility that they feel when anticipating what it will be like to face the music of having to tell their story of poor achievement can also drive them to productive work.* (p. 196)

Other benefits of this process noted by Hackmann (1996, 1997), Stiggins (1994), and Babar and Tolensky (1996) include

- Students engaged in self-evaluation are more highly motivated to produce quality work
- Students' skills of organization, leadership, and public speaking are strengthened
- Students are empowered to make improvement through the goal-setting process
- The responsibility for student achievement is shared between home and school
- The conference itself is a form of authentic assessment
- Students are given the opportunity to learn and practice self-evaluation skills
- Positive communication between parent and student is fostered
- A significantly higher percentage of parents attend student-led conferences
- Students' self-confidence and self-esteem are increased
- Students and parents have a clearer understanding of the expectations for student learning

This is an impressive list, and it aligns well with practices recognized as developmentally appropriate for the middle school years (NMSA, 1995). As we continue to unravel the process of student-led conferences, we hope you come to agree with the words of one of our parents:

> *These conferences are great! I'm impressed by (my child's) ability to reflect on his learning, his strengths, and his weaknesses. Keep it up! I really like the self-evaluation aspect of the conference. It is a great tool and can be a skill used throughout his school career.*◆

2.

Begin With the End in Mind

Ownership. Buy-in. It seems as if these two concepts are at the center of much of what we do at the middle level. In our practices and procedures we continually strive to seek better ways to encourage our students to both "buy in" to and accept responsibility for their part in the learning process. An important key in achieving this goal is to employ authentic methods of assessment. Stiggins (1994)) informs us that when we "...teach students to understand and demonstrate key dimensions of performance, we prepare them to achieve the targets we value." This in turn leads to higher academic performance and accountability. At Talent Middle School, the search for students' accountability in their learning led us to implement school-wide student-led conferences.

It began in the fall of 1993. Portfolios were used by a few of our language arts teachers to observe growth in writing over time. Some teachers used self-reflections to help students analyze their strengths and weaknesses as learners. That fall, conferences were held arena-style with parents scheduled for ten-minute appointments with a maximum of three teachers.

Two of the authors were frustrated with this process and were ready to try something else. They used portfolios and self-reflections to help students become more accountable for their learning, but they also felt something was still missing. Students were capable of doing quality work, but when asked to explain what they had learned, what their strengths as learners were, or what skills they needed to improve upon, they were unable to give clear answers.

After doing research on effective methods of assessment, we decided to give student-led conferences a try – and saw immediate results. Students zealously embraced the idea of doing their own conferences. The payoff? Students became much more responsible for completing assignments, more articulate in explaining work, and more accurate at analyzing themselves as learners. This, along with one-hundred percent participation by parents, sold us on student-led conferences.

Students eagerly prepare for conferences.

Over the next several years, increasing numbers of teachers joined in the process. Portfolios and self-reflections became an integral part of assessment at the school, and by the fall of 1996 every student and certified staff member (administrators too) were involved in student-led conferences.

Organization

There are several key decisions to be made if your school wishes to implement school-wide student-led conferences. Remember, your first year's organization is critical. A smooth, well-organized initiation into student-led conferences goes a long way toward convincing your staff, students, and parents of its many benefits. In creating a structure for your school, you must keep in mind the needs of your staff, your students, and your parents. Although every school's plan will differ somewhat, the elements discussed below are all ones that need to be addressed.

Purpose

Before you can determine when and how to hold a student-led conference, you must first answer the question "why?" Will the conference correct recognized deficiencies in the grading system? Are the conferences designed to show parents work in progress or to show progress toward a standard? Are the goals set at the conference for immediate implementation or implementation over time?

At TMS we hold conferences twice a year. In the fall, all of our students participate in a student-led conference designed to show parents work that emphasizes both process and product. We feel it is as important for students to address *how* they learn as *what* they learn. The goals that students and their parents set reflect this purpose and are often tied to students' learning habits and behaviors.

In the spring, we hold a more formal student-led conference for eighth graders. The purpose of this presentation is to show progress toward standards set by the state. Discussions center on how each student has (or has not) met the required benchmarks as measured by work samples and state tests. The goals set following this conference focus on the growth necessary to meet future standards requirements.

As you think through the implementation of this process at your school, answering "why" will help you determine the best format and organization for your conferences.

Facilitators

Who is responsible for facilitating a student-led conference? While students will play the key role in the actual conference, an adult should serve as the facilitator.

At Talent Middle School, each student is assigned an advisor to oversee Oregon's school reform efforts. Each teacher, administrator, and counselor is randomly assigned 18-19 students with equal numbers of sixth, seventh, and eighth graders. These students remain with the same advisor for their three years in middle school; each fall a staff member's eighth graders are replaced with incoming sixth graders and students new to the school. When we moved to school-wide student-led conferences, it was natural for us to use this system to facilitate the conferences.

Advisors/facilitators must also prepare for conferences.

While this system works for us, the following items must be considered if you choose to use a similar plan. First, since students are randomly assigned advisors, the advisor-facilitator of the conference may not be a current teacher of the student. In the beginning this was of great concern to some teachers, but as the years have passed it has become a lesser concern. Second, if everyone serves as an advisor, there is not always someone available to troubleshoot if the need arises. While infrequent, there have been times when it would have been helpful to have an administrator available to assist with a "sticky" situation. A possible solution to this issue is to have a district administrator present in the building.

Other possibilities for organizing facilitators include homerooms, advisory groups, teams, or choosing a set period (i.e. everyone facilitates his/her second period class). Look at your school's structure and see what is already in place that can be adapted, but be sure and consider the issue of equity in making your decision. If the staff feels that everyone shares an equal load, buy-in is less of an issue.

Timeline

Creating a timeline prevents those "unpleasant" surprises that can derail the process. Early in the school year, a small group of staff representing various areas should decide what needs to be done and when and who will be responsible for it. Success lies in the details. Nothing is too small to include – even picky things such as when the forms will be sent to the print shop or who will be responsible for making sure families are scheduled together. After the timeline is created, distribute copies to all those involved in the process. See Figure 2-1 for a sample.

FIGURE 2-1

Talent Middle School Student-Led Conferences
Timeline for Staff/Student Preparation

Sep 7-Nov 8	Teach, reflect, and gather sample work to use in conferences
October 4	Overview of conference plan with new teachers
October 11	Present overview of SLC plan to staff, share time line
	Departmental meetings to review cover sheets
October 20	Facilitator groups: Get acquainted, share system with new students
November 1	Student Services schedules sibling conferences.
	Cover sheets/missing work forms out to teachers
November 3	Facilitator groups: Schedule students, fill out postcards, return to office
November 8	Staff meeting to troubleshoot and discuss last minute details.
	Work prepared/practiced: Cover sheets, work, reflections, missing sheets.
November 10	LA teachers help students write Dear Parent letter. Send on collection days
November 9-10	Collection days for work. Give folder out 1st period. Drop off to conference facilitator – 6th period
November 12	Grades turned in by end of day. Morning inservice, afternoon for grades
November 15-19	Conference facilitators help students organize all work, fill in table of contents, and write goals. Teach and practice the conference procedure.
November 19	Conference facilitator: Report cards placed in folders. Send home reminder invitation. Final check to be sure all is prepared
November 22-24	**STUDENT-LED CONFERENCES!!!**
November 29	First day of new trimester
December 1	Case managers: Celebrate and have a "How did it go?" discussion
December 2	Students pick up conference portfolio from facilitator at beginning of 1st period. "Unload" file throughout day (some work may need to be kept; the rest can go home).

Schedule of meetings

When developing the timeline it is important to determine how often groups should meet together to work on the student-led conference process. If conference facilitators do not meet with their students on a daily basis, a special schedule will be needed for those days used to prepare for the conference. Starting with the conference and working backwards is an easy way to determine how much time is needed for preparation. In deciding your school's needs, think about how much time it will take to get acquainted and teach students about the process, how much time will be spent in organizing paperwork, in writing goals, and in actual practice.

Responsibilities

Clearly defining the responsibilities of the student, the conference facilitator, and the classroom teacher will help the process go smoothly. Since classroom teachers play two roles, it is important that they know what is expected in each of those jobs. For example, they should assign their students work that will lend itself to use in a conference, help their students select samples of work from their classroom portfolios, and give their students opportunites to practice sharing those pieces during class.

As facilitators, they schedule the conferences, help students organize their portfolios of work from all classes, teach students how to put it all together into a smooth presentation, and be present during the actual conference.

Student responsibilities should be spelled out as well. Students need to know it is their job to complete the required assignments, to self-evaluate their skills as a learner, collect the work and see that it is taken to the correct place, and prepare themselves to lead an effective conference with their parents or guardians.

Conference schedule

Creating a schedule that accommodates the needs of parents is complicated. Since we had parents and teachers who still wanted an opportunity to visit together during the conference days, we created a schedule that allowed for a thirty-minute conference followed by a thirty-minute "drop in" period. After the conference, parents who wished to visit with a particular teacher could do so. Our schedule runs for one eight-hour day, one twelve-hour day to allow for evening conferences, and one four-hour day.

Parent communication

To successfully implement student-led conferences in your school, parents must be informed of the process as well. Use any means possible to get the word out – school newsletters, letters mailed home, parent nights, articles in your local newspapers. Be creative! The more parents know and understand the process, the more willing they will be to participate (see Figures 2-2 and 2-3 for sample communication).

Staff development

As mentioned earlier, student-led conferences began at TMS as a grass roots movement by teachers. While the teachers and parents involved felt it was successful, moving it to a building level required careful planning. We knew it would not happen by accident. Like any effective teaching practice, it would take teaching, modeling, training, and refining. Once the decision was made by the school's site council to go school-wide, intensive planning began.

We began by assessing current school practices that would enhance the student-led conference process, and we found two major pieces already in place. Most of the staff already kept student portfolios of sample work and also had students write self-reflections to help evaluate themselves as learners and to set further learning goals. With these two practices in place, we could move forward on the details.

FIGURE 2-2

Article from Parent Newsletter

Student Led Conferences Set for November 23,24,25

On November 23, 24, or 25 all students at TMS will be scheduled to participate in a student-led conference. We have used this format for conferences over the past several years because we believe that student involvement in the conferences makes learning active, provides opportunities for students to self-reflect and evaluate their performance, and encourages students to accept responsibility for their learning.

In the process leading up to the conference, students will create a portfolio representing work over the first twelve weeks of school. The students will conduct the conference detailing skills and processes learned, as well as share goals they've set to further improve themselves. Students will be taught how to select representative work, how to write self-reflective evaluations, and how to diagnose their own strengths and weaknesses. Included in each portfolio will be a traditional report card.

A thirty-minute time block will be scheduled for you and your child to conference together. Your child's case manager (which, in most cases, is his or her e-lab teacher) will facilitate the conference. We feel this is an important experience for all students and hope for 100% participation.

Conferences will be scheduled from 7:30 a.m. to 3:30 p.m. on the 23rd, from 8 a.m. to 8 p.m. on the 24th, and from 7:00 a.m. to 11:30 a.m. on the 25th. For parents wishing to speak with specific teachers, a drop-in time will be available during the half-hour prior to and the half-hour following the conference.

We will schedule the conference the first week in November. You can help us by telling your child what day and time works best for you. A postcard will be mailed home to you to confirm your appointment. Thank you in advance for supporting your child's education in such an important way.

F<small>IGURE</small> 2-3

Conferences

Dear Parents,

During parent conference week this year, the district has scheduled <u>three full days</u> for conferencing: November 23rd, 24th, and 25th. Our classes will approach our conferences in a different way through an activity called student-led conferences. It is our belief that lifelong learners accept responsibility for their work. This includes student involvement to make learning active, to self-reflect and evaluate their performance, and to discover who they are as learners.

In student-led conferences, students create a portfolio representing work over the past ten weeks. A portfolio is a purposeful collection of student work that tells the story of his/her growth as a learner. Students will conduct the conferences detailing skills and processes learned, as well as the goals they've set to further improve themselves. Over the next two weeks in class, students will be taught how to select representative work for their portfolio, to write self-reflective evaluations to diagnose their own strengths and weaknesses, and to report their progress to you.

Since we know these conferences will take longer than the usual ten minutes scheduled, we have scheduled thirty-minute blocks of time and increased the times available to meet with you. It is a vital and important experience that all students are able to share with parents what they've learned. For this reason, we ask that 100 percent of our parents participate in these conferences. Please see your scheduled time below for your child's conference. If you need a different time, please call 535-1552 and ask for Kathy in Student Services.

We are looking forward to this experience. Thank you for supporting your child's education in such a meaningful way. If you have any questions, please call us at school or home.

Sincerely,
Pam Sessions
Mary Beth Munroe

Student-Led Conferences…Another Way to Learn

Your scheduled time for _____ is:

_____   _____   _____
Date   Time   Place

Remember to call if this time is not convenient. Since many of you will be scheduling conferences with other teachers during this week, we are scheduling our conferences before school-wide conferences are scheduled. You will receive information on the school-wide conferences in a week or so. In case you cannot coordinate the student-led conferences with the school-wide conferences, we hope some of you will not mind making an extra trip to TMS. We promise the experience will be worth it!

During our first staff training in the spring prior to fall implementation we presented an overview including

- A researched-based rationale for moving to student-led conferences
- Responsibilities of student, classroom teacher, and the facilitator
- The conference format we would use to maintain consistency
- A timeline of responsibilities/events leading up to the conferences
- A sample schedule

The next training began with a video of a student-led conference. The video had been made for training purposes using a capable student with two teachers playing the role of parents. As we progressed in our process, this was replaced by a video of actual conferences. At this time we also discussed the type of work samples that would be used during the conference. Experience had taught us that demonstrating multiple skills and processes was more effective than a piece of work demonstrating a single skill; for example, a research project was more effective than a spelling test. Teachers were asked to include appropriate work samples in their curricula.

Subject area meetings were encouraged. This led to more consistency in the type of samples being collected for each content area. Subject area teachers were also responsible for designing a cover sheet that would be used to rate learning behaviors of students in their classes.

Over the next several months, mini-training sessions took place on topics such as scheduling, self-reflections, how to have students collect work samples, portfolio organization, writing of "Dear Parent" letters, goal setting, and general conference procedures. We found it best to work from a "needs to know" philosophy of staff development. Rather than cover everything at once, we discovered it worked better to give a big picture overview and then teach the smaller pieces just prior to implementation. To some degree, this helped prevent the feeling of being overwhelmed. But, as when implementing any new idea, it was a challenge not to overstress the staff. It was not until the first round of conferences were completed that some of our staff members finally agreed that student-led conferences were much better than the arena-style conferences of the past.

Our best advice for training your staff is to *keep it simple*. Most of the procedures used in student-led conferences are just an extension of effective teaching practices currently in use. Remind them of this. Give as much support, modeling, and encouragement as possible and you will reap the rewards in the end! ◆

3.

Meanwhile . . . Back in the Classroom

As you consider the change to student-led conferences, it is important that you keep your primary task, that of educating students, at the forefront. When we began this conference format, our purpose was to enhance the good teaching we already did. With that in mind, once the initial steps for student-led conferences are in place, we spend the next several weeks focused on our curriculum and appropriate instruction.

As a classroom teacher, there are three separate but related tasks to help students prepare for the student-led conference:

- Plan ahead to teach content standards in ways that demonstrate multiple skills and processes
- Implement the curriculum so that work is completed and prepared for students to conference
- Help the students evaluate the work and discover what the evidence tells them about who they are as learners

Start to plan early in the year

We begin to prepare for conferences during the fall. As teachers design units, they look at the products and processes students can share by the time of the conferences. As always, state standards and district-adopted curriculum play a key role when we make these decisions.

Since our students need to discuss their learning in terms of skills and processes, work planned for a student-led portfolio should meet the following criteria:

Start early in the year to plan for student-led conferences.

- Show multiple skills and processes
- Address state/local curriculum standards
- Emphasize process as well as quality of product
- Use examples of "real work" not work contrived for show

We have found, through personal experience, that there are some thoughtful decisions to be made early in the year. These decisions make the actual conferences much easier.

Designing work samples

When designing work samples, among the questions that need to be considered are these:

1. Will the content be integrated or taught as single subjects?
2. Will teams work together or will each teacher act individually?
3. Can the work be completed in time for the conferences?
4. Are the conferences scheduled for the fall and/or the spring?

At our school, fall conferences tend to be for setting goals while spring conferences tend to be more summary oriented. However, goals *are* set at both types of conferences.

One of the immediate benefits of implementing student-led conferences was the focus the conferences gave students. Because they knew that all work would be collected and possibly used for conferences, an immediate rise in overall student performance was noted. Ever since that first powerful improvement, we have made sure to share with students that work is being gathered for that purpose. We also have learned to share the timeline for preparing for fall conferences so students realize they are major players in the success of this activity.

Once the curriculum has been designed, teachers utilize a variety of ways to instruct. It is really the teachers who are the heart and soul of successful conferences. They teach well, encourage students, and give ownership for the successes back to the students. While students realize that they will showcase their work at the fall conferences, teaching and learning take the driver's seat for the first two months. As each large project or piece of work is completed, we now have students' complete self-reflections to further clarify what has been learned. Students' reflections can also be used to clarify what has been learned by the class and what still needs to be learned for instructional purposes. Since there may be a discrepancy between taught and learned material, teachers are able to review key ideas needing further emphasis.

Portfolios and collecting work

There are many ways to manage collected work samples. The one that works for you will be based on your style, teaching environment, available space, and budget. Be sure to tell parents early in the year that work will not be sent home, but inform them that they may set up an appointment to see the contents of the collection folder at any time.

There are many possible containers for housing work samples and related items including the following three options:

Legal filing cabinet. This is the optimum storage solution. Have a drawer for each class. Students have their own hanging file to store a "Collection Folder." This is the storehouse for all work in the class. In order to make this easier on management, most teachers who use this system hand out graded work once every week or so for students to place in the file.

Plastic crates. This is an inexpensive way to store student work. The drawback is that usually two crates are needed per class to provide enough room. Work samples also have to be limited to a smaller size to fit within the crate's dimensions. Again, each student has a hanging file and a "Collection Folder" within the hanging file.

Banker's boxes. The cardboard boxes that come flat and are then assembled are an inexpensive way to gather student work. Have the students place their "Collection Folders" in the box after work has been added. The drawback is that files slide down and are hard to keep organized. Legal files can be used with these boxes, making larger work samples collectible. At least two boxes are needed per class.

When conference time nears, students pull the "Collection Folder" to choose the work for the student-led conferences. Since a portfolio is a collection of *thoughtfully chosen* work, the collection folder does not qualify as a portfolio. It is only when a student and teacher have pulled selected pieces that a portfolio is created.

The classroom – a few weeks until conferences

Two to three weeks before conferences, the pace of activities in our classrooms increases. All of our students begin to sort through the "Collection Folders" to choose work for the conference portfolio. The work chosen may be a mix of teacher-suggested pieces and student selections. Sometimes you may want to have all students include a particular unit of study because it illustrates a long-term learning process, but you might also let them choose which writing piece they think is the best example of their work. Discuss with your students the kinds of work that make suitable entries so they are better able to make good choices. Encourage each student to think through what they have learned and how to best show that learning to parents. Figure 3-1 outlines work sample criteria.

Once students have chosen the samples for their conference portfolio, the previously completed self-reflections should be reviewed reminding them of their own thoughts as they did particular work. Each student must complete summary reflections to show growth over time and significant skills learned. You need to teach your students how to share that particular work, giving them ample opportunity to rehearse. Teach students how to refer back to the work sample for evidence of the skills and processes learned. This might involve giving them a highlighter pen to mark a specific passage to share or putting stars next to particular comments on self-reflections that ought to be shared during the conference.

We understand that classroom work samples do not show all that needs to be addressed at a complete conference. When two of us piloted the early conferences, we asked students to complete a behavioral report card. This was a simple sheet addressing such skills of independence as turning work in on time, being on task in the classroom, joining into discussions, or treating others with respect. Now that we have gone school-wide, we designed a simple process to address this same concern in a variety of subject areas. Our students complete cover sheets for the subject areas represented in the portfolio. See Figure 3-2 and the section on Additional Forms and Handouts.

Each of our teams has designed a checklist of significant behaviors that lead to success in their particular subject, i. e., works with lab materials safely (science), reads regularly at home (language arts), or dresses down daily (physical education). Students rate themselves with a + or - on each behavior. Teachers also give a rating and then have a discussion with the student if there is a discrepancy. Interestingly enough, usually students are much harder at rating themselves than we would ever be! Most individual conferences are to acknowledge how well students are doing and to encourage them to rate themselves higher than they originally indicated. The cover sheets also have a place for teacher comments. These often are what we would tell parents if we met with them personally. The comments can be positive and/or negative as determined by student behavior. If necessary, a note can be written to encourage the parent to visit during the drop-in times.

The work samples collected in each subject are then stapled behind the cover sheet in a pre-specified order. This packet is now ready to be collected during the all-school collection time and taken to the facilitator's classroom for the final conference preparation. ◆

FIGURE 3-1

Student-Led Conference Work Samples

Better Choices: (focus on skills/process)
    Writing pieces
        -Including all drafts
    Science experiments
        -Including hypothesis, lab notes and findings
    Mathematics problem-solving
        -Including process, solution, and proof
    Applied mathematics
        -Designing house plans
    Book reviews
        -Including summary as well as review of author's style
    Research projects
        -Including notes and student created product
    Physical Fitness summary
        -Including pre and post skills and growth over time

Less Effective Work Samples: (focus on single skills)
    Spelling tests*
    Answers to chapter questions*   (*These can be included as
    Mathematics timed test*   student choice, but recognize
    Multiple choice tests*   how limited they are.)

FIGURE 3-2

Core

(Reading, Writing, Speaking, and Social Studies)

Name ___Mary_____ Teacher ___Mr. Smith_____

Behaviors of a successful student:

+ exceeds expectations   ✓ meets expectation   - needs improvement

Self	Teacher	
✔	_____	Completes classwork/homework on time
✔	_____	Works independently
✔	_____	Works well in a group
✔	_____	Manages behavior appropriately
✔	_____	Comes to class prepared to learn

Comments:

Mary is doing excellent work in her class group but is having a difficult time completing assignments and working on her own.

4.
Self-Reflections

A rt Costa (1989) said, "We must constantly remind ourselves that the ultimate purpose of evaluation is to enable students to evaluate themselves." It may be true that the essence of education is the ability to look back on the learning experience and evaluate what worked and why, and what didn't work and why not. We believe that asking students to reflect on their work should be a part of everyday learning and, therefore, we have made it an integral part of the conference process. Through self-reflections, students learn to develop insights into their learning and develop the ability to go beyond simply telling about the grade received on an assignment. Therefore, all pieces included in the student-led conference portfolio have been reflected upon in writing, with the reflection becoming a vital piece of information to be read and shared at the conference.

While closely related, it is critical to distinguish between self-evaluation and self-reflection. Self-evaluation occurs when a student assesses a performance against a standard in order to judge the quality of the performance. This may include using scoring guides or state or district standards. For example, a student may rate a piece of writing against criteria previously set. This is an important skill and necessary if students are to effectively present themselves as learners (Paulson & Paulson, 1994).

Self-reflection, on the other hand, focuses on understanding the learning process to help students discover what they have learned, how they learned it, and what they need to do next in order to extend and refine their learning. It involves self-knowledge about the performance, such as: What am I doing? Why am I doing it? What am I trying to achieve? Am I being successful? How can I change my performance in a desirable way? The focus of self-reflection is never negative, but encourages honest recognition of strengths, areas to work on, and subsequent goal setting (Smith & Ylvisaker, 1993).

By self-reflecting, students gain a greater appreciation of themselves and a stronger commitment to learning. As middle school students progress toward adolescence they can be empowered to assume greater responsibility for their learning. Students possess intimate information about their learning. Asking them to reflect on a piece of writing, a project, or their learning over a period of time, validates their self-knowledge and promotes a sense of collegiality between teacher and student.

Self-reflection is essential if we are to create a setting in which students take personal responsibility for their learning, analyze their successes, and identify those areas they want to improve. Helping students become more careful and observant players in their own learning takes them closer to becoming self-managed adults. Students in classrooms where self-reflection is a natural part of the curriculum have time to appreciate what they have learned and are then able to set realistic and achievable goals for improvement.

There are many effective and workable ways for students to analyze, evaluate, or comment on their work, thus self-reflections may look very different depending on the ability of the student and the particular classroom activity. To make self-reflections more meaningful and less of a "canned" activity, they should be varied in format and length. They may be written or oral and saved on paper, cards, drawings, diskettes, audiotapes, or videotapes. Students need to reflect on individual work, compare similar pieces of work, look at collected work over a significant period of time (a quarter, a semester, or year), and discuss growth and change. Students may also reflect on their learning in a specific subject area (math, science, social studies, reading) by looking at the skills and processes that are involved in that particular subject area. An important word of caution – self-reflections must not be overdone or students may react negatively and see self-reflection as busy-work. Use the process wisely and purposefully.

In many of our classrooms, teachers and students experiment with different forms of reflections until they find the ones that work best for them. Types of reflections may include

- Focused and highly specific questions students respond to in writing
- Drawing a picture or webbing the process one went through, what was learned, and what needs to be done differently next time
- Making a graph of the effort, satisfaction, interest, and value achieved from the project or assignment
- Letters to self or teacher
- Evaluative essays
- Checklists or charts
- Commercially designed reflection forms
- Teacher or student-designed reflection forms
- Class discussions, one-on-one conferencing
- Using journal entries and responding in learning logs
- Brainstorming

For students to become proficient at self-reflection, the process must be taught, modeled, and reinforced. Quality reflections take time. You will increase the value and depth of comments by allowing ample time for students to respond thoughtfully.

As students are taught to self-reflect they will become more revealing and better at recognizing and identifying patterns of their own performance (e.g., "I tend to procrastinate"), at taking ownership of their learning, and at using clear examples to support their thoughts by balancing generalizations with specifics. They will also make their reflections multi-dimensional by recognizing strengths and weaknesses, processes and strategies, or skills and knowledge.

Following are two examples of student reflections that illustrate writing and reading self-reflections. They can be used to show analysis of skills and processes, how skills and processes have changed over time, and how the affective areas of learning such as attitudes and beliefs may be addressed. Use these as starting points for designing self-reflections for your own students. ◆

FIGURE 4-1

Self-Reflection – Writing

First, look over the writing you have done this trimester then thoughtfully answer the questions below. Think of yourself as a writer!

---

1. What does someone have to do in order to be a good writer?

   To be a good writer you have to practice, have a good imaginative mind.

2. What is the most important or useful thing you've learned as a writer?

   The most important thing that helps me is to sit in a room with no noise and close my eyes and think.

3. What one thing in writing do you feel more confident about than you did at the beginning of the school year?

   I feel more confident about everything. I never have liked writing, but I think it's fun now.

4. What could you teach someone about writing?

   To not stop, keep going. Something will come up that you like.

5. Which writing trait is your strongest? Why?

   Ideas and content. I have great ideas that are unusual.

6. Which writing trait do you feel is your weakest?

   Voice. I am not good at doing anything with voice, I would like to work on it.

7. Which mode of writing do you enjoy the most/ Why?

   Narrative. I am not good at Imaginative. It is much easier to write about something that actually happend for me.

8. What still confuses you?

   Voice. I am not too good at any of the things with voice.

9. What can I (the teacher) do to help you be a better writer?

   Do more writing assignments.

10. What kind of writing would you like to do in the future?

    Narritive and persuasive.

11. What are your writing goals for the next trimester?

    I have a goal to improve voice on my writing assignments by using better words.

Figure 4-2

Self-Reflection -- Reading

First look over your reading responses, your list of books you have read, and your reading work. As you answer these questions, think about how you have grown as a reader this trimester.

What has been the most rewarding to you in the way we have reading workshop in our classroom? How has it changed you as a reader?

In this classroom it has been nice to read your own choise of a book and not reading a book together. It has changed me so I like reading more.

What are your strengths as a reader?

I think I have a strength in picking out books, I havent read a book I havent liked

What would you like to improve on as a reader?

I need to read more so I could be a faster reader.

What's the best book you've read this trimester?

Phantoms. It made me keep reading.

What makes this one of the best for you?

It was very exciting made me never want to put it down.

What's the most significant thing you learned from this book and/or discovered about yourself as you read it?

I learned that you have to ask questions sometimes to understand

What genres of books would you like to read in the future?

alot of Dean Koontz books

What can I (the teacher) help you do as a reader?

I would like more time to read

What goals do you plan for yourself as a reader?

to read alot faster and finish more books

5

Putting the Pieces Together

Think of a student-led conference as a giant jigsaw puzzle. A teacher's job is to design the pieces, the student's task is to create them, and now it's the advisor's turn to help students put the parts together to complete the big picture. Conferences need to be scheduled, students' work needs to be collected and organized, the "Dear Parent" letters must be written, goals must be set, and above all, students need to practice, practice, practice!

Scheduling conferences

Prior to scheduling conferences parents should be informed of the conference days and times. This can be accomplished by mailing a letter home, publishing the information in the parent newsletter, sending home a flyer with the dates and times indicated, announcing it to students in the daily announcements, or any combination of the above.

A scheduling sheet for each advisor is created showing times available for conferences and for drop-ins (see Figure 5-1). Siblings should be scheduled first. We compile a list of families, and personnel in the main office call the oldest child in the family down to schedule the conferences. Once this process is completed, schedule sheets are given to the advisor with postcards (see Figure 5-2) and mailing labels.

Approximately three weeks before the actual conferences, an advisory session is held to schedule all students. The advisor asks each child for a time that will work for his/her parents and schedules accordingly. Advisors are allowed to schedule themselves breaks during a conference time, but must be available in their rooms during the drop-in times. We schedule up to three conferences simultaneously during the day; if necessary, four during the evening session.

If students are unsure of a good conference time for their parents, advisors simply select a time. Since a message on the postcard informs parents to call the school if the selected time does not work, this method avoids lengthy delays and bouts of "phone tag" trying to find a convenient time. Absent students are scheduled in the same way. A postcard for each conference is then filled out with the correct time, date, and place. The mailing label is attached, and all postcards are returned to the office to be mailed.

FIGURE 5-1

MASTER SCHEDULE FOR: _Patti Kinney_ (Case Manager's Name)

MONDAY, NOV 22

Student's Name   Parent's Name

7:30-8:00 _SLC_ _____

7:30-8:00 _SLC_ _____

7:30-8:00 _SLC_ _____
    8:00-8:30 (Drop-Ins).........

8:30-9:00 _SLC_ _____

8:30-9:00 _SLC_ _____

8:30-9:00 _SLC_ _____
    9:00-9:30 (Drop-Ins).........

9:30-10:00 SLC _Amber_   _Ron & Kathy_

9:30-10:00 SLC _Jodi_   _Carol & Mike_

9:30-10:00 _SLC_ _____
    10:00-10:30 (Drop-Ins).........

10:30-11:00 _SLC_ _____

10:30-11:00 _SLC_ _____

10:30-11:00 _SLC_ _____
    11:00 - 11:30 (Drop-ins).........
    11:30-12:30 **Lunch Break** ....

12:30-1:00 _SLC_ _David_   _Jeff_

12:30-1:00 _SLC_ _____

12:30-1:00 _SLC_ _____
    1:00-1:30 (Drop-Ins).........

1:30-2:00 _SLC_ _____

1:30-2:00 _SLC_ _____

1:30-2:00 _SLC_ _____
    2:00-2:30 (Drop-Ins).........

2:30-3:00 _SLC_ _Jason_   _Ruth Anne_

2:30-3:00 _SLC_ _____

2:30-3:00 _SLC_ _____
    3:00-3:30 (Drop-Ins).........

24

FIGURE 5-2

TALENT MIDDLE SCHOOL
STUDENT-LED CONFERENCES

Dear Parents/Guardians:

You and your child have been scheduled for a conference on:

_____ _____ _____
       (date)   (time)   (room)

_____ _____
      (student name)   (case manager)

If you need to reschedule, please call Carol Tracy in student services at 535-1552. If you wish to speak with specific teachers a drop-in time will be available during the half-hour prior to and the half-hour following the scheduled conference. For those of you scheduled near a mealtime or at the end of the day, you may wish to call the school to confirm the availability of the drop-in time. Thank you!

TALENT MIDDLE SCHOOL
Conferencias dirigidas por los estudiantes

Estimados padres/guardianos:

La hora para su conferencia es::

_____ _____ _____
       (fecha)   (hora)   (lugar)

_____ _____
(nombre de estudiante)   (administrador/a)

Si usted necesita otra hora, favor de llamar al 535-1552 hable con Carol Tracy, servicios estudiantiles. Si usted quisiera hablar con un maestro/a especifico, habrá un periodo de tiempo libre de 30 minutos antes de y despues de la conferencia eligida. Los que tienen una conferencia cerca de la hora de comer o al fin del dia, deben llamar a la escuela para confirmar la asesibilidad de este tiempo.

Collecting work samples

The first step in putting together the conference portfolio is for students to gather their work in one place. For this to go smoothly a process must be created that allows students to transport their work from their teachers to their advisor. Your collection process will depend somewhat on your school's organizational structure. If your school is organized by teams, this can be done fairly simply with students taking their work to the designated team member. Another way is to give students a folder (a large sheet of manila paper folded in half) during their first period class. Students carry the folder with them during the day, adding work from each class. Five minutes before the end of the day, students are dismissed so they can take their folders to their advisor.

Organizing the work

A table of contents provides a clear and consistent structure for students to organize their portfolios and allows parents to follow the presentation. To complete this step, students put their work in the order listed on the table of contents and write the name of the assignments in the appropriate places (see Figure 5-3).

Missing work

How do we deal with missing or incomplete work? We copy Figure 5-4 on a bright color (astrobright pink works well), have students fill it out, and put it in the place of any missing work. We discovered that students do not like to have this paper in their portfolios and will frequently finish or find the missing assignment. It's not unusual for a student to come running up to his advisor and demand immediate replacement of the missing work page with the actual assignment.

Some people may question accepting late work, but we decided if a student takes the initiative to find or complete the work, we would accept it for conference use. However, that does not mean the classroom teacher is required to accept it for full or even partial credit; we leave that decision up to the teacher.

Writing the "Dear Parent" letter

Frequently, the most difficult part of a presentation is simply getting started. By giving students this tool to use as an "ice breaker" we are helping set them up for success. Using a standard friendly letter format, students write a letter to their parent(s) or guardian(s) welcoming them to the conference, telling them about the contents of their portfolio, and explaining what they will share with them during the conference. Letters tend to be creative, expressive, and personalized (see Figures 5-5 and 5-6 for sample letters). This letter can be written under the direction of the conference advisor, but since letter writing is a natural part of language arts, we have our students write these letters under the instruction of their language arts teacher.

FIGURE 5-3

Table of Contents
Fall Student-Led Conferences
Talent Middle School

Name: David   Date: Nov. 10 1999

- Dear Parent Letter

- Core (Reading, Writing, Social Studies) Cover Sheet

    - ABC BOOK / Elements - Devices
    - Personal Narrative
    - Country Study Project
    - Essay - Honduras

- Mathematics Cover Sheet

    - Chapter Test - Notes
    - Problem Solving - Pizza Geometry

- Science or Health Cover Sheet

    - Literature Circles - The accident
    - Decision Tree's

- Elective Cover Sheet

    - Practice Chart - Band

    - _____

- PE or 2nd Elective Cover Sheet

    - Fitness Testing

    - _____

- Report Card

- Goals for Success

- Parent Homework

FIGURE 5-4

Missing Work!

Student Name: <u>Caroline</u> Teacher Name: <u>Mrs Munroe</u>

Assignment Title: <u>Character Report card</u> Subject: <u>Core</u>

Assignment Due Date: <u>10 - 25 - 99</u>

I was given the opportunity to do this work but either did not complete it or turn it in because:

<u>I swear I finished it, it</u>
<u>just didn't make it to the school!</u>
<u>First of all, my brother being such</u>
<u>a klutz, spilt juice all over it. Trying</u>
<u>to dry it off, I stuffed it in the</u>
<u>dryer, which wasn't too smart. After going</u>
through 2 rolls of scootch tape, I still couldn't
get it into one peice, so I just gave up!
I promise I'll turn it in next time!

Examples of "Dear Parent" Letters

FIGURE 5-5

> 11-12-97
>
> Dear Mom,
>   Welcome to my mindblowing portfolio. You will be seeing my mostmagnificent work from various classes. These classes are Science, Math, Band, Core and P.E. I'm really excited that you will get to see my divine piece of writing that I did in Core.
>   My greatest strength is that I work independently. My greatest weakness is I don't always get my work in on time.
>   Thank you for coming. I hope you learn from all this that I work really hard.
>
>   Love,
>   Galen

FIGURE 5-6

> Dear mom and Dad
>   In this portfolio are some samples of my work from school.
>
>   Even though I haven't been here long, I have done lots of work, some are good examples and some I still need to work on.
>
>   a subject I like alot is math with mrs. Ganoys. Another subject is keyboarding with mrs. Stratton. I also like mr. Neat in core. I dont have a lot of work to show, but have learned alot since coming to talent middle school.
>
>   Love,
>   your daughter,
>   Shelly

Goal setting

Once students have organized their work and written their "Dear Parent" letters, it is time to review their work to begin the goal-setting process. This is such a critical piece in the conference that we have dedicated a chapter to the process. So, refer to Chapter 6 for more information on setting effective goals.

Parent homework

Middle school students love the idea of giving their parents a homework assignment. Since one of the goals of a student-led conference is to foster better communication between students and parents regarding progress in school, the parent homework assignment was created. At the end of the conference students give their parents an assignment sheet (Figure 5-7) asking them to respond to the conference in writing. This "assignment" is optional and may or may not be returned to the teacher. The responses are often very touching and meaningful to the student (see Figure 5-8).

Teaching the process

Helping students see the overall process they will follow during the conference sets the stage for practicing the conference in advisor groups. We teach our students to use the following steps:

- Introduce your parents to your advisor
- Explain to your parents that you will share work collected from the first 12 weeks of school
- Briefly review the Table of Contents to give your parents an overview of what is inside your portfolio
- Read your "Dear Parent" letter
- Present your work following the order in the Table of Contents. For each subject, explain the cover sheet, how you scored yourself, and how your teacher scored you
- Share information about each piece, what it is, what knowledge and skills you learned, and the process you went through to complete it
- Read aloud all or key portions of your self-reflections
- Explain the two goals you have set
- Write the third goal with your parents
- Explain to your parents what they need to do for the Parent Homework Letter
- Thank your parents for coming

Once students understand the steps to this process, it's time to practice. We begin by showing a video of a student giving a portion of a student-led conference. In the absence of a video, another way to begin the practice session might be to have a student present her portfolio to her advisor in front of the class.

FIGURE 5-7

PARENT HOMEWORK

...g in your child's conference .... now you have some homework.

...ive personal note about the conference. Below are some areas you

...s you write:

...hat I noticed about your work was …

...vas proud of you for …

...eep up the good work on …

...know you have difficulty sometimes, but …

...'m glad you are making an extra effort in …

...How can I help you?

We hope this experience was as rewarding to you and your child as the process was to us. Thanks again for taking the extra effort!

Sincerely,

Talent Middle School Staff

FIGURE 5-8

Dear Kara,

Thank you so much for working so hard on your conference. We were delighted to be able to come to your classroom and see all the things that you have done so far this year. I know that you have enjoyed being in Middle School and are looking forward to a lot more fun!

I was very impressed with your ability to speak to us about your accomplishments in your core class. You were very organized, and seemed to feel comfortable talking to us about something other than everyday family matters. I know that speaking in front of a small group can be a scary thing - but you did a fine job.

Both of us (Mom and Dad), are very proud of your school work. You are able to take on a challenge and do a good job. It was evident that you are concerned about doing well at school - your papers, projects and grades reflect a very positive feeling of self motivation. This is a wonderful trait to have, as it will help you along in many different ways throughout your life.

We want to encourage you to keep up the good work, positive attitude, and smiling face. Those things will make your life easier - in your studies, and in the day to day "stuff" that will come your way.

All in all Kara, we were so pleased with your conference we were about to burst with pride. You are a wonderful and important member of our family, and we love you very much!

With love, Mom and Dad

Breaking students into groups of two or three seems to be the most effective way for students to practice the conference. Emphasize creating a smooth presentation that flows easily from one section to another; remember, students have already had the opportunity to practice their pieces separately in their subject area classes. Each student in the group takes turns presenting his/her portfolio to other students. Changing groups for each practice session keeps students' interest at a higher level.

How long does this process take? We generally schedule four or five days of 35 minute sessions for the students to work with their advisors on goal setting and practicing the conference. At the end of practice sessions, students fill out a final invitation (Figure 5-9) to take home as a reminder for the conference, and then they are ready for the next step – successfully leading the conference! ◆

FIGURE 5-9

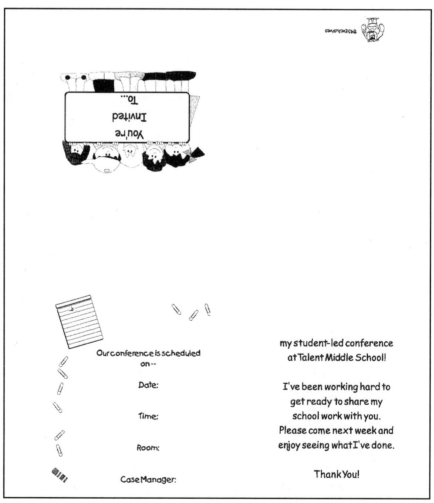

Directions: Fold in half and then again with the page "You're Invited To" as the outside cover.

6.

Setting Goals for the Future

Portfolios and student-led conferences are part of a larger purpose – improving student performance. Crucial to achieving this outcome is the goal-setting process. This step provides an opportunity for students to analyze their strengths and growth areas and develop an improvement plan that empowers them to take charge of their own learning. However, to be truly effective, goal setting must be done in a supportive environment. Using student-led conferences and making goal setting a joint venture involving students, families, and school leads to stronger and longer two-way communication between home and school.

Talent Middle School parent Kelly Moran agrees. When asked what she liked best about student-led conferences, she responded

> *You involve your student with the goals. They get to be involved rather than a teacher or parent talking about what they want for the child; you bring the child into the whole process. They're setting goals for themselves and then they are more apt to keep the goals that they have set for themselves. They are also setting them with the people who are there to help them accomplish those goals. It's important to the student and important to the teachers also. He's able to see his strengths and weaknesses and he's held accountable with the people who are there to help him improve and do better. He sees his own strengths and weaknesses and is able to see where he is now and where he needs to be by the end of the year and where he needs to be in his life. I think that's the best thing.*

Goal setting must be designed to help students develop clear, specific steps to succeed as learners. In our student-led conference model there are three steps to this process: setting preliminary goals before the conference, sharing the goals during the conference (including creating one in collaboration with parents), and finally, revisiting goals regularly to assess and revise for further success.

Step One: Setting goals before the conference.

To begin the goal-setting process our students use knowledge gained through the self-reflection process to choose three strengths and three areas for improvement. Most students find this process easy, but if your students struggle with this, have them re-read their self-reflections and identify strengths and areas of growth that may have been suggested. From this information students then choose three areas to develop goals.

To be successful in meeting these goals, students need to choose objectives that are clear, specific, and achievable. We encourage students to select a mix of academic and behavioral goals. Often it is a behavior that keeps some students from being successful. For example, procrastination and talking are two areas that regularly come up with middle level students. How nice it is when they recognize and set a goal to work on these issues. We find that students who have reflected on their work in a thoughtful manner often come up with the goals we would have chosen for them.

It is harder for students to define actions necessary to achieve their goals. Teachers can assist students in breaking the goal into clear, measurable steps. First, ask students to think of a general goal, for example, "I want to write better," then using this idea students specify what they need to do in order to accomplish this goal. An example would be, "I need to work on writing sentences that flow and sound natural when read aloud." The students then decide on two things that they can do to accomplish these goals. For instance, to meet the above goal, a student might decide to have another student read aloud his paper so he can "hear" the flow of his writing, and to read aloud papers to himself, his parents, or a friend to "hear" the flow of his sentences.

Asking students to write their goals increases the likelihood that they will change their behavior. Reading the goals aloud to a significant person makes this likelihood even stronger. We ask students to choose two of their goals to write on the NCR form (see Figure 6-1). The third goal is held until the actual conference where it is used as the backup when setting a third goal with parents. The final pre-conference goal step is to list people who can help with attaining the goals and noting distractions that may inhibit success.

Step Two: Sharing the goals

The day of the conference arrives. Before sharing goals with parents students show work from all classes and discuss the skills, processes, and content learned. Key points from the self-reflections are also shared leading naturally into the goal-setting part of the conference. Prior to this time, the conference facilitator has remained in the background to allow a natural conversation to develop between students and parents. At this time the conference facilitator rejoins the discussion to become part of the goal-setting team.

The student begins by sharing strengths and the areas in which she needs to improve. From there, the first two goals are shared along with the plan for achievement. Parents are invited to help refine the goals and action plan if necessary. The third goal is a collaborative effort by the goal-setting team. At this point the student asks her parents if they have a third goal in mind. If the parents draw a blank, she suggests the backup goal set aside earlier. Together, an action plan for achievement is created and written down (see Figure 6-2). Parents are then asked to review the list of helpers and distractions the student created earlier and suggest any additions.

FIGURE 6-1

TMS Goals for Success

Name _Michael_   Date _11/19/97_

My strengths are:
A. Being descriptive in my writings.
B. Getting work done on time in science
C. Turning in my practice chart on time in band

I need to work on:
A. Not socializing with my friends.
B. Using teamwork in P.E.
C. Cooperating with my lab partners.

First Goal _Not to socialize with my friends when I'm not allowed to._

To achieve this goal, I will
A. Sit by people I won't talk to.
B. Ignore them if they talk to me.

Second Goal _I will try to cooperate with the partner I'm assigned to._

To achieve this goal, I will
A. I will let them try the stuff I would want to try.
B. I will try to get better at getting along with different people.

Third Goal _____

To achieve this goal, I will
A.
B.

People who can help me attain these goals are: Mom, teachers, friends, and myself.

Distractions that may get in the way of accomplishing these goals are: T.V., my sister, and friends.

Michael   _Patti Kinney_
Student Signature   Parent Signature   Case Manager Signature

WHITE COPY-PARENT   YELLOW COPY-CASE MANAGER   PINK COPY-CORE TEACHER

FIGURE 6-2

TMS Goals for Success

Name: Michael   Date: 11/19/97

My strengths are:
A. Being descriptive in my writings.
B. Getting work done on time in science
C. Turning in my practice chart on time in band

I need to work on:
A. Not socializing with my friends.
B. Using teamwork in P.E.
C. Cooperating with my lab partners.

First Goal: Not to socialize with my friends when I'm not allowed to.

To achieve this goal, I will
A. Sit by people I won't talk to.
B. Ignore them if they talk to me.

Second Goal: I will try to cooperate with the partner I'm assigned to.

To achieve this goal, I will
A. I will let them try the stuff I would want to try.
B. I will try to get better at getting along with different people.

Third Goal: If I don't understand my work I will get help instead of skipping it.

To achieve this goal, I will
A. Ask for help.
B. Ask the teacher to help me.
C. Try to explain it to someone else.

People who can help me attain these goals are: Mom, teachers, friends, and myself.

Distractions that may get in the way of accomplishing these goals are: T.V., my sister, and friends.

_____   _____   _____
Student Signature   Parent Signature   Case Manager Signature

WHITE COPY-PARENT   YELLOW COPY-CASE MANAGER   PINK COPY-CORE TEACHER

By signing the goal sheet, all members of the goal-setting team make a commitment to help the student work toward success. The original copy is sent home with the family with a suggestion to place it in a prominent spot – possibly the refrigerator door. The other two copies are kept at school, one with the conference facilitator, the other with the student's language arts (or homeroom) teacher.

Step Three: Revisiting goals

Feedback is important in achieving goals. Dates must be set for periodic reviews of progress – both at home and in school – towards accomplishing the previously agreed upon goals. Home reviews will probably be less formal, but they will provide students and their parents a chance to revisit the goals together and discuss progress toward meeting the goals. By revisiting their goals teachers and/or parents can help ensure that students develop the necessary skills and knowledge to successfully reach their goals and set new ones.

At progress report time (midway through the next trimester) our students meet with their conference facilitator. The original goal sheets are reviewed – sometimes with laughter. Using a three-part NCR form (see Figure 6-3), students indicate progress (or lack of it) toward their goals. Often the action plan is refined or even completely changed to help students continue to meet the goals. If a goal has already been achieved, a new goal is identified. This revisitation process helps students learn to be accountable for meeting goals by monitoring their own progress on a regular basis. The original copy of the "goals – revisited" page is then mailed home along with the student's progress report. One copy is kept by the conference facilitator, the other copy is sent to the language arts (or homeroom) teacher.

Teachers assist students with breaking the goals into clear, measurable steps.

We have found that goal setting is the "heart" of the student-led conference process and is the piece that truly empowers students to accept responsibility for their own learning and growth. Psychologist Mihalyi Czikszentmikaly (1990) has made an interesting discovery about the connection between goals and happiness: Goals are the stuff of motivation, persistence and well being. He discovered that what people enjoy most is pursuing a clear, doable goal that they value. Goals are essential to student improvement. ◆

FIGURE 6-3

Goals for Success -- Revisited

Name _Michael_   Date _1/23/98_

Mrs. La Tourette

First Goal _Not to socialize with my friends when I'm not allowed to._

List two things you have done (or are doing) to meet this goal.

1. _I am sitting by people I won't talk to._
2. _I'm ignoring people that do talk to me._

What are two things you can do (or continue to do) in the next few weeks to make sure you are successful in meeting this goal?

1. _I can ask the teacher to help me sit in a good plac_
2. _I can ignore people that try to talk to me._

Circle the word that describes your effort to date in meeting goal 1:   None   Little   Some   (Good)   Excellent

Second Goal _I will try to cooperate with the partner I'm assigned to._

List two things you have done (or are doing) to meet this goal.

1. _I will try to let them do stuff that I would want to do._
2. _I'm trying to get better at getting along with different people._

What are two things you can do (or continue to do) in the next few weeks to make sure you are successful in meeting this goal?

1. _I'm continuing to get along with different people._
2. _I will try to let them do stuff I would want to do_

Circle the word that describes your effort to date in meeting goal 2:   None   Little   (Some)   Good   Excellent

Third Goal _If I don't understand my work I will get help instead of skipping it._

List two things you have done (or are doing) to meet this goal.

1. _Asked for help._
2. _Asked the teacher to help me._

What are two things you can do (or continue to do) in the next few weeks to make sure you are successful in meeting this goal?

1. _Ask for help._
2. _Try to explain it to someone else._

Circle the word that describes your effort to date in meeting goal 3:   None   Little   Some   (Good)   Excellent

White copy - Parent   Yellow Copy - Case Manager   Pink Copy - Core Teacher

7.

The Conference

The big day has arrived. As students and their parents enter the building, they are met by a staff member or parent volunteer who offers coffee and information. As they continue down the hallway, you can almost hear the wheels turning as students run through a final practice in their minds. The classroom they enter has been organized to accommodate up to four simultaneous conferences. Tables are set apart from each other with the chairs arranged for maximum privacy.

Lane: Mom and Dad, I would like you to meet my teacher, Mrs. Munroe. Mrs. Munroe, these are my parents, Teresa and Mike.

Mrs. Munroe: I'm glad you're here. It's nice to meet you. If you'd come over here we have the conference all set up so we can get started. Lane, if you'll sit in the middle. What we've found works best is if the parents sit on each side. I'll just briefly explain how this conference is going to look. It may be a bit different than other conferences you've attended.

First of all, Lane knows what he's going to say and he's going to be sharing his work with you. He'll share what he has found out he's good at, and also what he knows he's not as good at. I'll be in the room and come back near the end when he's ready to share his goals. That way I can listen in so I can help him achieve his goals too. Other than that, he's the one running the conference.

At this point the parents and their child sit together at a table. The student is in the center, one parent on either side. The portfolio is ready and waiting on the table. The teacher fades into the background and lets the student take over.

The student takes over the conference.

Dad: Sounds good. Are you ready?

Lane: No (with a laugh) but here goes. Mom, Dad, this is my portfolio, and I'm going to sit here and I guess I'll start. This is a letter that I have written to you guys to introduce you to my portfolio.

> *Dear Mom and Dad,*
>
> *Whew, the trimester is almost over and yes, I have learned a lot. This portfolio has some of my best work (even though I only have best work – yeah, right). (laughter)*
>
> *I hope you enjoy seeing my growth through this trimester and I can even see some improvement in my own work. My favorite piece in this folder is my descriptive writing that you will soon see. I've seen growth in my schoolwork and I hope you do too.*
>
> *If you have any special questions for any of my teachers, you can stop by their rooms and visit with them during the drop in-period.*
>
> *Love, your son Lane*

Mom: Great!

The "Dear Parent letter" has served its purpose. The ice is broken and the conference is off to a good start.

Lane: This is my reading list and these are the books that I've read this trimester.

Dad: What does this mean?

Lane: This is the rating for the different types of books. You rate the book between 1-5 on the best level of what it is and how much you liked it. And then…

Mom: So this one that's got a 6++ must mean you really liked it.

Lane: Yeah, I really loved that one.

Dad: So, that doesn't necessarily indicate how difficult it is to read.

Lane: No, that's here. Difficulty is easy, average, hard.

Dad: Oh, I see.

Lane: This is one of my first responses for this year and I feel it is one of my best responses. It shows that I can evaluate and predict. And I did pretty good on it.

Mom: Can I ask a question? In response to what?

Lane: It's a response to a book that I read during that day.

Mom: Oh, okay.

Lane: Like what you read about – if you feel any connections between your life and what the character or someone in the book is feeling.

Mom: Sort of like a daily journal.

Lane: Yeah. This is my book project on Gary Paulsen. I figured out this year that I liked him a lot – his style of adventure. He's not just a phony writer; it could be reality – and most things are based on his experience. This is my reading self-evaluation. The number of novels I've read so far this year is five and two of the ones I liked a lot are *The Foxman* by Gary Paulsen and *The Voyage of the Frog* – and I'm not sure at this moment who wrote that one.

Mom: This is the one you had as a 6++.

The conference continues as Lane moves into a section on social studies. He shows his parents the work he has completed while studying ancient Greece and concludes by summarizing his accomplishments.

Lane: These are my requirements that I have fulfilled during this project on ancient Greece. Here are some of the things I did. I communicated through writing, speaking, visual forms, and some other stuff. I've been a self-directed learner by trying to stay focused. I've used technology and computers and some other things. I've also shown I'm able to interpret literature.

In Lane's conference, work from his health class comes next.

Lane: This is my book we had to write for health about alcohol and what can happen if you use it. I wrote a "choose your own adventure" book.

Mom: I remember when you worked on that.

Lane: Yeah, you guys helped on this. It tells about the kinds of choices you can make, like if you accept a drink of alcohol or not…and on my reflection for it "what was the hardest part of the project?" I said, "Making up the story because I had a hard time deciding on what to write and how to say it." And for "If I could do this project again, what would I do differently?" I wrote, "I'd change it to an alphabet style book, like A is for alcohol, B is for booze, and have little stick figures doing something to illustrate each letter."

Mom: Well, I like the way you did it!

The math section begins with an explanation of the cover sheet.

Lane: This is my math section and my teacher is Mrs. Bostwick and I'm in Math 4. For having materials in class and being ready to work, I gave myself a check plus and she scored me a plus.

Dad: Good

Lane: "Is responsible for assigned tasks" we both marked a check. For "makes a positive contribution to class" we both marked a plus.

Mom: Great.

Lane: And her comment was "Lane is a good student and does well in math."

Mom: Thanks to his dad!! (laughter)

An in-depth conversation about his math work is followed by a discussion of what has been happening in physical education.

Lane: In PE we did a self-reflection on the trimester. We had to choose an activity that we did and explain three rules. I chose basketball and the rules are… Then we had to tell if we followed the rules honestly and I put "mostly" because sometimes I tend to foul a little bit, but sometimes that's expected!

Mom: Sounds like something you can work on.

Lane: This is my "missing work" page because I didn't do my make-ups when I had a dentist appointment a while back.

Mom: How does that affect PE?

Lane: I lose 5 points from my total for each make-up I don't turn in. It won't matter much 'cause I only did it once. So I'm fine.

At this point the conference moves into goal setting and Mrs. Munroe joins the group. Prior to this, she has worked quietly in the room, helped another conference group get started, and finished a discussion on goals with another student.

Lane: My strengths are that I understand math concepts pretty well, I can read fast and have a high vocabulary, and I can follow directions well. What I need to work on are spelling words, talking too much, and waking up on time!

My first goal is that I will not be as social in class. To achieve this goal, I will be quiet when I'm told to, listen well, and look at the teacher to show I am paying attention.

My second goal is that I will watch TV one hour or less on weekdays – I want to cut my watching time. To achieve this goal I'll read more in my spare time and participate in more sport activities.

Dad: I'd like to comment that I think you're already working on and making good progress with this goal. You have increased your reading three- or four-fold – and it's making a difference.

Lane: I need your help in writing a third goal. Do you have any ideas?

Silence for a few moments.

Mrs. Munroe: You've looked at his work and you've seen him at home. He's shared goals he feels are important and he has an idea for a third, but is there one that you feel would help him not only be a better student but learn something you feel is important for him to know?

Mom: One that is more life skills than academic is dealing with anger management – finding healthier ways to vent teen frustrations.

Lane: How could I write that – manage my anger?

Mom: Maybe handle your emotions in a positive manner.

Mrs. Munroe: So how could you do that?

Lane: Well, I already do sports and that helps me work out some of my feelings.

Mom: How about identify the source of anger or frustration? That way you put it in it's proper place rather than take it out on someone else.

Mrs. Munroe: Does that make sense to you?

Lane: Not really.

Mrs. Munroe: It sounds like she's saying you tend to react to outside things. It's like I go home and I kick the dog – but I'm not really angry at the dog.

Mom: Yeah, you come home from school and something has happened and you take it out on all of us by yelling and being in a bad mood.

Lane: Okay, that makes sense to me. People who can help me are family, friends, and teachers.

Dad: What will get in your way?

Lane: Maybe watching too much TV or spending time on the computer.

The conference wraps up a few minutes later when Lane explains the parent homework assignment to his mother and father. He hands his parents an evaluation form and asks them to turn it in near the school entrance. As they leave the room, they say good-bye and decide which teachers they should visit during the drop-in time. ◆

8.

Where Do We Go Next?

Celebration

Give yourself a pat on the back and celebrate! Putting together a successful round of student-led conferences is hard work and deserves recognition. Acknowledge staff contributions to the process, bring in treats, have a social time, and just relax when it's all over.

And don't forget the students. They also deserve to be recognized for their efforts. After student-led conferences in the fall, we generally bring in donuts or ice cream bars for all students and let them know what a good job they did. In the spring, when our 8th graders finish their benchmark presentations (a more formalized version of student-led conferences to show progress toward meeting state standards) all students who completed their presentation are taken to a skating/dance activity arranged just for them.

Evaluation

Just as students are taught to evaluate and reflect on their work, teachers need to do the same with the student-led conference process. Looking at the conferences from the perspectives of the staff, parents, and students will give you an overall picture of the process and help you see where both major readjustments and minor refinements should be made.

Staff feedback

It is critical that the teachers in your school feel that their concerns are heard. If your school is like ours, it is likely that you did not have one hundred percent, enthusiastic buy-in for your first attempt at student-led conferences. Change is difficult for many people and stepping outside their comfort zones can be troubling. Ask staff for feedback in writing (see Figure 8-1) and analyze it carefully. Often, a few minor adjustments in the logistics can have a tremendous impact on your colleagues' perceptions about the process.

Parent feedback

Feedback received from parents can also be very beneficial for improving the process. Parents have not been as involved in creating and implementing the process as staff and students, so they look at it from a different perspective.

FIGURE 8-1

Staff Evaluation of Student-Led Conferences

We would like everybody to complete this form in the next few days. By Thursday, please put the completed form in the envelope by Judy's desk and check off your name.

Years you have done SLC's (this was our 4th year of school-wide conferences)

❏ 1st year   ❏ 2nd year   ❏ 3rd year   ❏ 4th year   ❏ 5 or more

Using a scale of 1 (poor), 2 (okay), 3 (fine), 4 (good), 5 (very good), 6 (excellent), how would you rate the overall process and format.

1   2   3   4   5   6

Please indicate your thoughts on the following areas. <u>If you indicate "needs work," please give details and suggestions for improvement.</u>

1. Your knowledge of process (knew expectations, dates, process, etc.)
   ❏ no problems
   ❏ needs work

2. Preparation of student work in the classroom (knew expectations, due dates, etc.)
   ❏ no problems
   ❏ needs work

3. Scheduling process (office does families, case managers do postcards, etc.)
   ❏ no problems
   ❏ needs work

4. Schedule used (times, drop-ins, evening schedule, schedule own breaks, etc.)
   ❏ no problems
   ❏ needs work

5. Collection of work (use of paper folder, students collect work over two days, etc.)
   ❏ no problems
   ❏ needs work

(FIGURE 8-1, CONTINUED)

6. Table of Contents and "Dear Parent" Letter — we changed the process this year. Case managers were responsible for helping students organize and get the table of contents filled out (core teachers used to be responsible) and core teachers had students write the "Dear Parent" letter.
   ❑ no problems
   ❑ needs work

7. Writing of goals
   ❑ no problems
   ❑ needs work

8. Process for practicing in case managers (amount of time, use of video, etc.)
   ❑ no problems
   ❑ needs work

9. Notification of changes in conference schedule
   ❑ no problems
   ❑ needs work

10. Other: Please comment on any area not addressed above. Thanks!

During our first year of student-led conferences, every parent was given an evaluation form (Figure 8-2) at the end of the conference and asked to complete it and turn it in near the front door as they left the building. We found the comments were extremely positive for the most part; but in reading them, it became clear where we had not given enough clear information. For example, many parents seemed confused about the purpose of the drop-in visits and several commented they would like to have had time to speak with their child's teacher.

The next year, we made sure that the information about drop-in opportunities was published in the school newsletter and written on the post cards mailed home to confirm the conference appointment. Subsequently, drop-in time was more effective and caused less concern. As parents become more familiar with the process, it may not be necessary to ask every parent to fill out an evaluation form. Some years, instead of giving the forms out at the end of the conference, we simply have them available near the front door.

FIGURE 8-2

Talent Middle School Parent Questionnaire
Student-Led Conference

Parents,

Thank you for coming. Hope you enjoyed your visit. Please take a moment to answer the following questions before you leave.

TMS Staff

Please circle the number that corresponds to whether you agree/disagree with the statement.

1. My child was prepared for the conference.
    Strongly disagree   Strongly agree
           1   2   3   4   5

2. I now have a better understanding of how my child learns.
    Strongly disagree   Strongly agree
           1   2   3   4   5

3. I have a clear picture about what my child has been studying this trimester.
    Strongly disagree   Strongly agree
           1   2   3   4   5

4. I have a better understanding of my child's effort, study skills, and classroom behav-
    iors.
    Strongly disagree   Strongly agree
           1   2   3   4   5

5. The student-led conference was valuable and informative.
    Strongly disagree   Strongly agree
           1   2   3   4   5

6. My child wrote goals that will help improve his/her performance.
    Strongly disagree   Strongly agree
           1   2   3   4   5

7. Additional Comments:

Student feedback

Middle school students can be brutally honest and are quite willing to give their opinions when asked. In our first few years of student-led conferences we asked all of our students to give us written feedback about the process (see Figure 8-3). However, experience has taught us that we get information (with less resistance) that is as rich, if we simply have a class discussion about what went well and what didn't go as well. This discussion works very well if combined with a celebration complete with treats.

FIGURE 8-3

Post Conference Thoughts

Things went smoothly during the conference because…

Things could have gone better if… ·

One thing I wish I would have shared with my parents, but forgot.

One thing I chose not to share, but should have…

The best thing about this experience was…

Anything else??

Making adjustments

After all the feedback has been compiled, it's time to make decisions on the next steps. Don't put this off until later; it's much more effective while the conferences are fresh on everyone's mind and people remember why they felt something worked or did not work. A strategy that works well for us is to create a small committee with representatives from all areas or teams. Have this group look at the information carefully. Are there consistent trends or just a few isolated concerns? Decide on which issues can be realistically handled and plan for the appropriate adjustments. Another decision that might be made at this time is how frequently to conduct conferences. Some schools with fall conferences choose to do them again in the spring, others do not.

For student-led conferences to be successful, evaluation must be an on-going process. Yearly evaluations to determine what needs to be refined are critical. These refinements will help you adapt the process to fit your school and thus help you better meet the needs of the community you serve. ◆

9.

Going It Alone

This chapter is included for those teachers ready to try student-led conferences, but who do not yet have the support or resources to begin a school-wide initiative. Here, two of the authors share their stories.

The yellow folder sat in the center of the table with three chairs in a row. The hot cider was brewing in the next room and the cookies were on a tray. I was ready to facilitate my first student-led conference, but I was nervous. Three months of planning and preparation had gone into this day. Kara came to the door with her parents. I noticed that she had chosen to dress nicely for the occasion. The formal introductions went smoothly. I showed them all to their seats and briefly discussed the new format. I stepped out to get the refreshments and let Kara begin on her own.

Kara pulled the opened the folder and read her "Dear Parent" letter. Relaxed laughter at a comment she had made followed me into the next room and I breathed a sigh of relief. The kids *were* prepared and the conferences were going to be successful. As the family left, Mrs. Leever stopped me. "Thank you for the most comfortable and informative conference we have ever had. I learned so much in this half hour about Kara and the things she has learned. I hope more teachers do conferences this way."

There are many reasons teachers decide to implement student-led conferences. For two of us it was a natural progression of creating a student-centered classroom. Both of us were using scoring guides to inform students of grading criteria, integrating the curriculum so it made more sense to the middle school learner, and providing choice through a reading-writing workshop model. After taking these steps, it seemed hypocritical to then sit across from parents and talk "about" student progress – with no student present.

We had been introduced to the student-led conference concept the year before at an integrated curriculum workshop. The positive effects of empowering students to set their own learning goals while creating an environment for child and parent to have a rich educational discussion seemed too good to ignore. We jumped in, like we always do, with both feet, and the results exceeded our wildest hopes. One-hundred percent of the parents attended. Students from learning disabled to gifted did a wonderful job, and parents and children left the conferences with smiles and pride.

SOOooo .... how did we do it? The steps are almost the same as outlined earlier in this book. Communication is the key. Parents, colleagues and students all must be aware of the process and how it impacts them. Our first action was to sit with the principal and seek support, an easy task when all of the benefits were shared. A harder task was to decide how to step out of the arena conferencing the rest of the staff still used. Instead of ten minutes to talk to parents who requested a conference, we would now have the luxury of 30 minutes for each student to share his/her progress. Since this would increase our total time spent conferencing, substitutes were hired so that we could have an extra day. Our principal requested to be kept informed of our progress as we prepared and asked us to design an evaluation form for parents to fill out at the end of the conference to measure their attitudes and support of the process. Now we were ready to go public!

Both of us typically write an introductory letter to parents early in the fall. The first year we included a paragraph stating that conferences would look a bit different. We explained that students would lead the conference, using their own work to show progress. It was also made clear that work samples are housed in a collection folder and so less work would be sent

Student buy-in is the key to successful conferences.

home. To alleviate fear of "surprise" grades, parents were invited into the classroom to view this work at any time. They were reassured that if a problem occurred before conferences, we would contact them.

Student buy-in is the key to successful conferences. The first week of school, the conference style was shared with them. To show them what it might look like we made up a mock portfolio containing a "Dear Parent" letter, work samples, self-reflections and goals. Students became very aware they would share their work over the next several weeks. As a result both of us noted an immediate improvement in students' quality of work. Our classes were also proud to have been "selected" as a pilot group. They became personally invested in the success of the student-led conference process.

The final early step necessary for us was to carefully consider our curriculum and classroom set-up. We did long-term planning to make sure that before conferences students would have a variety of writing samples to choose from, an in-depth reading task, and a social studies unit that included everything from vocabulary and maps to research and analysis. One of our "ah-has" at the end of our first year was that we had students put too many items into the portfolio. Quality and depth are better than quantity and single skill evidence.

We set up a work sample collection system. For us, the easier and simpler, the better. We each had a legal filing cabinet. One drawer was dedicated to each class and each student had a hanging file with a manila folder. As work was completed throughout the grading period, it was filed in the cabinet by the student. To keep this really simple, we saved graded work and passed it out once every week or so. This whole process became routine and our students could do it in about five minutes, filing several assignments simultaneously.

Student empowerment is necessary for successful student-led conferences. We taught our curriculum as we always had, except we spent a bit more time being sure students were aware of the criteria for grading and the purpose of each task. It is extremely important to help students know what they are learning! The process of self-reflection was taught at the end of larger, significant projects. We modeled self-reflections that had depth and thoughtful, insightful responses.

We had fun teaching and learning together from the initial introduction to student-led conferences through the final steps. When the time for our pilot conferences neared, communication again became important. Another letter was sent to parents giving a detailed explanation of what the conference style would look like. Parents would still attend the arena conferences for their child's other classes, so we scheduled a time for their student-led conference prior to their time with the other teachers. We allowed for changes but were pleasantly surprised to find very few occurred. The first year we scheduled only one conference at a time because it was important for us to see how things went before we tried two or three simultaneously.

Understandably, our students were a bit nervous at the task ahead of them. As teachers, we wanted them to be reassured and confident as they shared with their parents. The process of choosing work, organizing, and writing goals was the same as outlined in Chapter 5.

We found our students had significant buy-in because of the opportunity to self-select some of the pieces to share. While we knew the social studies unit was mandatory for all of the class because of the skills demonstrated, we could let students pick their strongest pieces from all of their writing samples. We also had a spot in the table of contents for student choice. Students were able to insert a minor piece that had great value to them such as a spelling test, a reading response, or a creative poem. This blend of teacher and student selection for portfolio contents helped students recognize the value of such work and contributed greatly to the project's success.

The first year, both of us had our students over-practice the conference because it was so important that they be successful. We outlined a conference format, modeled it for them, and then let them practice with peers for several days. We explained the importance of being side-by-side rather than across from their parents. Students practiced holding on to their work while explaining it so parents didn't take it away while they were pointing out certain points. They learned to talk about what was shown by the work rather than just what the work was. By the time they conferenced with their parents, it was very easy for them. In the next few years, we found that students who had participated in a student-led conference previously needed much less practice time (once or twice was often sufficient).

After the introduction and explanation of the conference, we left the child alone at the table with parents to get started. By the time we returned with refreshments, they were usually laughing over a comment in the "Dear Parent" letter and the conference was off to a great start. We would sit at a desk or table behind the conference and listen as we did quiet work. Unless a question came up, we remained there until the goals were being written. Then we rejoined to listen to the goals of the student, encourage the parents to help set a third goal, and bring closure to the conference. To end the conference, parents were given an evaluation and the parent homework assignment.

Both of us met in the hall shortly after our first conferences. We were as excited as kids. *Magic* had happened! The students had been incredible. Parents were so impressed with what they learned and left smiling. Shy students did an excellent job because they felt comfortable with their parents. Students with IEPs did fine because they were finally able to point out what they can do instead of what they can't.

It was fun! We had 100% of our parents turn out for the student-led conferences, even those who generally avoided the arena conferences attended. The depth of conversation between middle school students and the parents was impressive. Our students had exhibited a strong belief that they were in charge of their own learning and had written goals in areas they had personally identified. When the goals were revisited in six weeks, we found many had been met or were clearly in the process of being met.

Despite the amount of time and effort it took to implement this by ourselves, we walked away totally convinced it was the only way to hold parent conferences. ◆

10.

Commonly Asked Questions About Student-Led Conferences

1. Can low-achieving students conduct effective conferences?

In our experience, the vast majority of low-achieving students do well with the student-led conference format. In fact, preparing for a student-led conference often motivates low-achieving students. If a student does not achieve because of behavioral reasons, the responsibility and ownership given to her in this conference setting usually causes a student to complete assignments and put more effort into those that are completed. For many of these students, this is the first time they have been given a voice to discuss their own learning.

If the student is low-achieving due to a learning disability and currently has an IEP, the self-reflections allow that student to highlight the strengths he has and set goals that are achievable for him. Our teachers work closely with the special education teacher throughout the year to be sure instruction is appropriate to each student. This also holds true in choosing appropriate samples for students with IEPs to place in the portfolio. In this setting, each student strives for his own best, not to reach a standard set by others. We have had mentally disabled students participate in this conference format. It is sometimes necessary, with this type of student, for the facilitator to remain throughout the conference in order to help the student focus on what to discuss and how to support with work samples.

2. What happens if parents don't attend?

In our school we have a plan to deal with this eventuality. First, the parent is called and the conference is rescheduled, if possible. Infrequently, but on occasion, a parent will not respond to this request. Since the rewards of this model come from the process of preparing for the conference and then having a caring person listen and support the student with the goals, we have found staff members willing to sit in lieu of a parent. The staff member can be anyone from a favorite teacher to the secretary to an instructional aide who has a relationship with the student. Since it can be difficult to schedule a staff member's time, other "listeners" can be volunteer parents. We have had many parents volunteer to sit in as surrogate parents for a conference.

3. How does an ESL conference work?

Our school has a significant percentage of English as a Second Language students. Often the parents of these students do not speak English at all. Student-led conferences have increased the number of parents who now attend. Those parents are not native English speakers. Because they know the communication is with their own child and in their primary language, and much less intimidating, they attend. Since the student is well prepared, it is not necessary for the facilitator to be bilingual. However, we attempt to place our ESL students who speak little English with a facilitator who speaks their native language. This helps with the preparation of the portfolio and the practice. The ESL students are better able to understand what they are going to tell their parents when the conference is taking place. Goals are often written in the native language so parents understand and support the students in achieving goals. If the non-native language speaking facilitator sits in for this portion of the conference, students are the translators, empowering them to take charge of their own education.

4. How is a student with high absenteeism successful?

There are many reasons for a student to be chronically absent. An ill child can be tutored to stay current with classroom assignments, including conference preparation. If the absenteeism is due more to apathy or a problematic home situation, the conference reflects this. The student must fill out "Missing Work" forms and discuss why there is little or no evidence of growth. Often this student's goals reflect study habits and attendance plans. By empowering students to look at their performance and decide what needs to be done about it, at-risk students are more likely to create improvements in their lives in spite of external factors.

5. How do we bring a reluctant teacher on board?

Change is hard for everyone. It is important for the leaders to listen to the concerns of the staff. We started small with a few teachers willing to pilot the student-led conference model. Their success was contagious, so the next year more teachers tried it. By the third year, when it was mandated school-wide, teachers were given the training and materials they needed. Most of the grumbling was ignored since the success of previous years showed that teachers would have to see it to believe it. We also were willing to "give in" on small logistical considerations in order to keep the basic philosophy intact. This give and take helped us achieve support from the staff and they were willing to give it a try.

6. With so many demands on teachers already, where do I find time to prepare?

With early planning, the actual extra classroom time is not as much as you'd think. Self-reflections should be written as major writings, projects, and units are completed. Have a system set up to hold finished work until conference time. Then the week or so before conferences students should gather this work and do summary reflections that address broad goals for each subject area. Yes, the conference preparation is greater than for an arena style conference, but the benefits are far greater.

7. How much preparation time does it take to get ready?

It is possible to do most of the preparation for the conference as part of regular teaching. For instance, it takes about 20 minutes after a major project to complete a self-reflection. Gathering work, organizing the portfolio, writing the goals, and practicing presentations is done for about thirty minutes a day during the seven to ten days before the conference. The more prepared a student is, the smoother the conference and usually, the greater the benefit. The time spent is also a good investment, because after goal-setting, more students follow through to complete work, do their homework, and come to class prepared to learn.

An important note: The ease of implementation for the classroom teacher is greatly increased if there is someone in the building who acts as an overseer for the logistics. This person would ensure necessary materials are printed for everyone, schedule siblings on the same day, and keep staff aware of the timeline. At TMS, our principal does this with some responsibilities delegated to the counselor, the media specialist, or other key support staff.

8. How do we satisfy parents' requests for parent conferences?

It is important to remember that the primary purpose of a conference is communication between home and school. We remind our parents that there is teacher drop-in time before and after the student-led conference for one-on-one communication with teachers. For most parents, this fills their needs. Parents who still want a conference with a teacher should be scheduled with one. Do not let this take the place of the student-led conference. The purpose of a parent-teacher conference is very different than a student-led conference. In order not to confuse the two, schedule parent conferences the week prior or the week after student-led conferences.

9. How do we handle parents who are aggressive or negative during the conference?

It is rare, in our experience, to have a parent act negatively toward her child in the conference. On those infrequent times when this has occurred, the facilitator joined the conference and redirected the discussion back to the purpose, empowering the student to take control of her education. That has always been effective. If a parent did persist in berating a student, we would even halt the conference so that emotional damage was not done. The safety of the student is the responsibility of the facilitator. This parent might need a one-on-one meeting with the teacher to have issues diffused. The student would complete the conference in a safe environment at a later time. We have not yet had to halt a conference because of an adversarial parent.

10. How do I enlist the support of my principal?

If at all possible, first get yourself a like-minded colleague to work with. The process is much easier to implement if you have someone to share the frustrations and joy of student-led conferences. Discuss with your principal what you would like to accomplish and how this will help your students make progress toward the goals of your school. Ask if you can pilot a program for your school and present a plan of how it would work and how you would evaluate its success. Be specific about what you need in order to implement the plan and be prepared to "give" lots of extra hours to make it succeed. Generally, after seeing it in action, administrators (and other teachers) see the value and are willing to support the process.

11. What kind of work is best to include in a conference folder?

Any type of work may be used in a conference, but we have found the most effective work demonstrates multiple skills and processes, addresses your state or district curriculum standards, is "real" work as opposed to "busy" work, and/or shows progress over time. Some examples include writing pieces (including early drafts), science lab write-ups, open-ended problem solving in mathematics, research projects, fitness summaries, and other assignments with relatively authentic assessments. Examples of less effective samples are vocabulary tests, answers to chapter questions, timed tests, and other "one point in time" assessments.

12. How often do you have contact with parents?

Our first organized contact with parents is a Back to School Night held the first few weeks of school. This provides an informal opportunity to meet parents and, if needed, begin to prepare them for student-led conferences.

We also encourage all of our teachers to be in regular contact with parents, especially if the student is not successful in that class. This includes notifying parents of missing work, inability of students to grasp concepts, and/or behavioral difficulties in the class. In regard to student-led conferences, we explain our process through the school newsletter and have letters sent home from individual teachers. Parents are then notified of conference times through post cards mailed home two to three weeks prior to the conference.

Since student-led conferences are also used in our elementary schools, parent education is not as intense as it would be if our students were doing it for the first time. If you are the first school in your district to initiate student-led conferences, we recommend you send several written notices home as well as hold an informational evening for interested parents. The more parents understand the intent and process of student-led conferences, the more supportive they will be.

13. How should the room be arranged for conferences?

Since you may have three or four conferences taking place at one time, room arrangement is important. We have found the most effective organization is having one station set up in each corner of the room. Each station consists of a small table with four or five chairs. Place the chairs with their backs to the center of the room to give a sense of privacy for each of the conference groups.

14. Who facilitates the conference?

As the adult in the room, the conference advisor is there to provide support, make sure the conference gets off to a good start, and step in to help the student only if the situation becomes difficult. After the initial introductions, the advisor should move out of the way and allow the student to run the conference. If possible, the advisor should rejoin the conference to assist during the goal-setting process.

15. Why should the facilitator step away for most of the conference?

Since the purpose of the student-led conference is to give a student an opportunity to share his work and his abilities as a learner, the student needs to be in charge of the conference. If the facilitator remains at the table that may inhibit the student. When we have remained at the table, we found parents would often turn to us to ask questions, leaving the student out of the process. Experience has taught us that students do much better on their own.

16. How do I deal with a problem student in a conference format?

It's amazing how well students rise to the occasion of student-led conferences. All of us have had experiences with a student who "goofed off" during practice and came through in the end, but that doesn't make it any easier if a student is uncooperative during practice time. If that situation occurs, we recommend you approach it as you would approach a difficult student in your classroom – talk with the student in private, give reminders and redirections, or contact parents if appropriate. If you have a difficult student and you would like to confer with the parents in addition to the student-led conference, you can use the cover sheet comments to ask the parents to visit you during a drop-in time.

17. How often do students meet with the facilitator to prepare?

This varies depending on the format you use for the conference. At our school, we meet for 35-minute periods in our conference advisor groups about seven or eight times prior to the conference.

18. Why do all of your certified staff act as facilitators?

We asked all certified staff to act as facilitators in order to reduce the size of each group. Another plus is that all certified staff have a clear understanding of the process and feel involved. Additionally, most non-teacher certified staff (counselors, media specialists, others) enjoy the opportunity to work with a group of students and build long-term relationships with them. The downside is that there are times, especially in the evening schedule, when no appropriate person is available to help with a problem. We found it helpful to invite a district office administrator to be on site at this time.

19. How did you find time to develop this process?

Inservice time is critical if this process will be successful. We are fortunate in our district to have a one-hour delayed start dedicated to staff training on Monday mornings. Prior to implementing this process, review your inservice calendar to see where time is available. In several districts we have worked with, the school principal approached the superintendent for permission for an early release afternoon to plan the process.

Since time is essential, be sure that whatever time you do have is productive. Be organized and have specific goals for each meeting. Having a plan to use as a starting point goes a long way toward ensuring that time is used effectively.

20. When is the best time to hold student-led conferences?

The time of the conference depends on the purpose for the conference. Fall conferences focus on growth to occur during the remainder of the school year and have the advantage of

- Providing students with a focus and direction early in the year
- Allowing students an opportunity to demonstrate their efforts at the beginning of the year
- Supplying parents with important information about both their child and the school
- Giving plenty of time for implementing goals

Spring conferences serve more as a summary and a celebration and are helpful because they

- Show a student's growth over time and emphasize accomplishments
- Emphasize important accomplishments made during the year
- Give a clear picture of the child's academic progress
- Allow for goals to be set for the next school year

One is not necessarily better than the other; they are simply done for different reasons. In making the decision about when to hold conferences, you must determine your purpose before setting your dates. ◆

References

Allen, J., & Little, N. (1990). *Student-led teacher conferences.* Toronto, Canada: Lugus Productions.

Association for Supervision and Curriculum Development. (1997). Using assessment to motivate students. *ASCD Education Update, 39* (8).

Austin, T. (1994). *Changing the view: Student-led parent conferences.* Portsmouth, NH: Heinemann.

Baber, S., & Tolensky, L. (1996). Student led conferences [On-line]. Available: http://www.yrbe.edu.on.ca/~cecn/slc/home.htm.

Benson, B., & Barnett, S. (1998). *Student-led conferencing using showcase portfolios.* Thousand Oaks, CA: Corwin Press.

Cleland, J. (1999). We can charts: Building blocks for student-led conferences. *The Reading Teacher 52* (6), 588-595.

Countryman, L. L., & Schroder, M. (1996). When students lead parent-teacher conferences. *Educational Leadership 53* (7), 64-68.

Cromwell, S. (1999, April 26). Student-led conferences: a growing trend. *Education World.*

Culver, L., & Cousino, G. (2000, January). Building a partnership: Student-led conferences engage students in evaluation of progress. *Schools in the Middle,* 13-15.

Czikszentmikaly, M. (1990). *Flow: The psychology of optimal experience.* New York: Harper Perennial.

Daniels, L. (1998, November 3). New method puts student in charge. *Portland Oregonian.*

Farber, P. (1999). Speak up: Student-led conference is a real conversation piece. *Middle Ground 2* (4), 21-24.

Grant, J. M., Heffler, B., & Mereweather, K. (1995). *Student led conferences using portfolios to share learning with parents.* Ontario, Canada: Pembroke.

Hackman, D.G. (1996). Student-led conferences at the middle level: Promoting student responsibility. *NASSP Bulletin 80* (578), 31-36.

Hackman, D.G. (1997, May). Student-led conferences at the middle level Eric Document Reproduction Service, No. ED 407171.

Hayden, L. (1998, Fall). Letting students lead parent conferences. *Middle Matters Newsletter.*

Holland, H. (1997). The highs and lows of parent-teacher conferences [On-Line]. Available: http://www.middleweb.com/CSLV2TchrConf.html.

Murphy, S., & Smith, M. (1980). *Writing portfolios: A bridge from teaching to assessment*. Portsmouth, NH: Heinemann.

National Middle School Association. (1995). *This we believe: Developmentally responsive middle level schools*. Columbus, OH: Author.

Paglin, C. (1996). Caity's conference: Kids show their stuff at student-led parent conferences. *Northwest Education 2* (1), 19, 35

Paulson, F.L., & Paulson, P.R. (1994, August). Student-led portfolio conferences. Eric Document Reproduction Service, No. ED 377241.

Picciotto, L. P. (1996). *Student-led parent conferences*. New York: Scholastic.

Servis, J. (1999). *The power of self-assessment and student-led conferencing: Celebrating the fourth: ideas and inspiration for teachers of grade 4*. Portsmouth, NH: Heinemann.

Smith, M., & Ylvisaker, M. (Eds.) (1993, September). *Teachers' voices: Portfolios in the classroom*. Berkeley, CA: National Writing Project.

Stiggins, R. J. (1994). *Student-centered classroom assessment*. New Jersey: Prentice-Hall.

Stiggins, R. J. (1999). Assessment, student confidence, and school success. *Phi Delta Kappan, 81* (3), 191-198.

Additional Forms and Handouts

W e have included the following section to give you starting points for creating your own forms and handouts. In it you will find a variety of self-reflections, cover sheets, and other forms used in the student-led conference process as well as memos used to inform our staff of the "details."

Student Procedures for Conferencing

1. Introduce your parents or guardian to your case manager.

2. Explain you will be sharing your fall portfolio during the conference.

3. Briefly review the Table of Contents to give an overview of what is in your portfolio.

4. Read your "Dear Parent" letter.

5. Present your work.
   Share the information on the cover sheet
   For each piece share:
   ⇒ What the assignment was
   ⇒ What knowledge or skills you learned by doing it
   ⇒ What process you went through to complete the piece
   ⇒ Key portions of your self-reflection by reading them aloud

6. Share your report card with your parents.

7. Goal Setting
   Explain the two goals you have set
   Write a third goal with your parents

8. Parent homework letter
   Give your parents their "assignment sheet" and ask them if they would be willing to write you a note as explained on the sheet. What they write can be kept at home or returned to school to put in your portfolio.

9. Closing
   Thank your parents for attending your conference.

Table of Contents
Fall Student-Led Conferences
Talent Middle School

Name: _____   Date: _____

- Dear Parent Letter

- Core (Reading, Writing, Social Studies) Cover Sheet

    - _____

    - _____

    - _____

    - _____

- Mathematics Cover Sheet

    - _____

    - _____

- Science or Health Cover Sheet

    - _____

    - _____

- Elective Cover Sheet

    - _____

    - _____

- PE or 2nd Elective Cover Sheet

    - _____

    - _____

- Report Card

- Goals for Success

- Parent Homework

Contents of
Student-Led Conferencing Portfolio

<u>Table of Contents</u> (lists all items in portfolio – filled out in core class)

<u>Dear Parent Letter</u> (serves as an icebreaker, introduces parents to conference, written in core)

<u>Worksamples</u>
    Core Cover Sheet (completed in core class by both teacher and student)
        2 to 4 samples of core class work with self reflections

    Science or Health Cover Sheet (completed in science or health class by both teacher and student)
        1 or 2 samples of science or health class work with self reflections

    Math Cover Sheet (completed in math class by both teacher and student)
        1 or 2 samples of math class work with self reflections

    PE Cover Sheet* (completed in PE class by both teacher and student)
        1 or 2 samples of PE class work with self reflections

    Elective Cover Sheet* (completed in elective class by both teacher and student)
        1 or 2 samples of elective class work with self reflections

        *Some 8th graders will have two electives and no PE

    Missing Work – Any uncompleted work should be indicated by a "missing work" form to be
        filled out by the student in class.

<u>Report Card</u> (This will be given to case managers on the Friday before conferences begin)

<u>TMS Goals for Success</u> (completed in case manager group)
        All students should have two goals and plan for accomplishment written on their goal sheet.
        Students will write 3rd goal in conjunction with parent during the conference. Students should have
        a 3rd goal and plan ready to use in case parents do not have one to suggest. For easy "access" his
        goal could be written down on the inside of their portfolio folder.

<u>Parent Homework Letter</u> (given to case managers for students to place in their folder)
        This is self-explanatory. Parents are encouraged (but not required) to respond to their child's
        conference in writing.

Core

(Reading, Writing, Speaking, and Social Studies)

Name _____ Teacher _____

Behaviors of a successful student:

+ exceeds expectations   ✓ meets expectation   - needs improvement

Self   Teacher

_____   _____   Completes classwork/homework on time

_____   _____   Works independently

_____   _____   Works well in a group

_____   _____   Manages behavior appropriately

_____   _____   Comes to class prepared to learn

Comments:

TMS MATH

Name: _____

Teacher: _____

Course: _____

Class Expectations:	Ratings:	Student	Teacher
Responsibility for Assigned Tasks:		_____	_____
Classroom Behavior:		_____	_____

Key to Ratings:

+ Exceeds expectations   ✓ Meets expectations   - Needs improvement

Comments:

  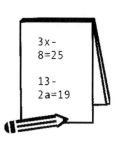

$3x - 8 = 25$

$13 - 2a = 19$

 # TMS Science

Name: _____

Teacher: ☐ McNichol   ☐ Schofield   ☐ Russo

Title of Work: _____

Class Expectations	Ratings:	Student	Teacher
Works well with lab partners		_____	_____
Works safely with lab equipment		_____	_____
Stays on task and completes work		_____	_____

Key to ratings:
    + exceeds expectations   ✓ meets expectations   - needs improvement

Comments:

Health

Name _____

Teacher _____ Class Period _____

Class Expectations	Ratings:	Student	Teacher
1. Works well independently		_____	_____
2. Works well with others		_____	_____
3. Completes assignments on time		_____	_____
4. Uses time wisely in class		_____	_____
5. Has a positive attitude		_____	_____
6. Treats people with respect		_____	_____

Missing assignments:

Key to Ratings:

   + Exceeds expectations   ✓ Meets expectations   - Needs improvements

Comments:

TMS
Electives

Name: _____

Teacher: _____

❏ Art/Crafts   ❏ Band   ❏ Choir

❏ Computers   ❏ Journalism

❏ Applied Math/Sci (Tech)   ❏ Aide

❏ Spanish   ❏ Intro to Languages

Class Expectations:	Ratings:	Student	Teacher
Shows respect for others, self and property		_____	_____
Stays on task to complete work		_____	_____

Key to Ratings:
    + Exceeds expectations   ✓ Meets expectations   - Needs improvement

Comments:

PHYSICAL EDUCATION
TEACHER/STUDENT EVALUATION

LEVEL OF COOPERATION WITH OTHER STUDENTS:

STUDENT:	1	2	3	4	5	6
TEACHER:	1	2	3	4	5	6

EFFORT (PARTICIPATING TO THE BEST OF ABILITY):

STUDENT:	1	2	3	4	5	6
TEACHER:	1	2	3	4	5	6

MAKE-UP FOR ABSENCES TURNED IN:

STUDENT:	1	2	3	4	5	6
TEACHER:	1	2	3	4	5	6

DRESSED DOWN DAILY IN PROPER UNIFORM :

STUDENT:	1	2	3	4	5	6
TEACHER:	1	2	3	4	5	6

LEVEL OF HONESTY AND FAIR PLAY (SPORTSMANSHIP):

STUDENT:	1	2	3	4	5	6
TEACHER:	1	2	3	4	5	6

ON TIME TO CLASS AND SEATED ON ASSIGNED ATTENDANCE NUMBER:

STUDENT:	1	2	3	4	5	6
TEACHER:	1	2	3	4	5	6

LISTENING SKILLS / FOLLOWING DIRECTIONS:

STUDENT:	1	2	3	4	5	6
TEACHER:	1	2	3	4	5	6

GOLDEN RULE - DO I TREAT OTHERS THE WAY I WOULD LIKE TO BE TREATED?

STUDENT:	1	2	3	4	5	6

SCORING GUIDE CONTINUUM

6/EXEMPLARY — Work at this level is both exceptional and memorable. It shows a distinctive and sophisticated application of knowledge and skills.

5/STRONG — Work at this level exceeds the standard. It shows a thorough and effective application of knowledge and skills.

4/PROFICIENT — Work at this level meets the standard. It is acceptable work that demonstrates application of essential knowledge and skills. Minor errors or omissions do not detract from the overall quality.

3/DEVELOPING — Getting there! Work at this level does not meet the standard. It shows basic, but inconsistent application of knowledge and skills. Work has minor errors or omissions that detract from the overall quality. It needs further development.

2/EMERGING — Work at this level shows partial application of knowledge and skills. It is typically superficial, fragmented or incomplete and needs considerable development before reflecting the proficient level. Work at this level may contain errors and omissions.

1/BEGINNING — The work shows little or no application of knowledge and skills. Work at this level contains major errors or omissions

NAME: _____

PERIOD: _____   DATE: _____

Missing Work!

Student Name: _____   Teacher Name: _____

Assignment Title: _____   Subject: _____

Assignment Due Date: _____

I was given the opportunity to do this work but either did not complete it or turn it in because:

_____

_____

_____

_____

_____

_____

TMS Goals for Success

Name _____   Date _____

My strengths are:
    A.
    B.
    C.
I need to work on:
    A.
    B.
    C.

First Goal _____

_____
To achieve this goal, I will
    A.
    B.

Second Goal _____

_____
To achieve this goal, I will
    A.
    B.

Third Goal _____

_____
To achieve this goal, I will
    A.
    B.

People who can help me attain these goals are:

Distractions that may get in the way of accomplishing these goals are:

_____   _____   _____
Student Signature   Parent Signature   Case Manager Signature

Goals for Success -- Revisited

Name _____ Date _____

First Goal _____

_____

List two things you have done (or are doing) to meet this goal.

1. _____

2. _____

What are two things you can do (or continue to do) in the next few weeks to make sure you are successful in meeting this goal?

1. _____

2. _____

Circle the word that describes your effort to date in meeting goal 1:   None   Little   Some   Good   Excellent

Second Goal _____

_____

List two things you have done (or are doing) to meet this goal.

1. _____

2. _____
What are two things you can do (or continue to do) in the next few weeks to make sure you are successful in meeting this goal?

1. _____

2. _____
Circle the word that describes your effort to date in meeting goal 2:   None   Little   Some   Good   Excellent

Third Goal _____

_____

List two things you have done (or are doing) to meet this goal.

1. _____

2. _____

What are two things you can do (or continue to do) in the next few weeks to make sure you are successful in meeting this goal?

1. _____

2. _____
Circle the word that describes your effort to date in meeting goal 3:   None   Little   Some   Good   Excellent

White copy - Parent   Yellow Copy - Case Manager   Pink Copy - Core Teacher

Scheduling Student-Led Conferences
Wednesday, Nov. 3

You will be scheduling your conferences on Wednesday during case manager time. For those new to the process, the easiest way to schedule is to call one student back at a time while having the rest of the class work quietly on something. Channel 1 will be shown. While not necessary, some have found it helpful to write the student's appointment time and day on a piece of paper so they can give their parents advance notice. Schedules and Postcards will be in your boxes on Wednesday morning. **Please review the following information before scheduling your conferences:**

⇒ Official times for conferences are:
- ⇒ Monday   7:30AM – 3:30PM   (lunch 11:30 – 12:30)
- ⇒ Tuesday   7:30AM – 8:00PM   (lunch 11:30 – 12:30, dinner 3:30 – 5:00)
- ⇒ Wednesday   7:30AM – 11:30PM
- ⇒ You have the option of scheduling a conference at 7:00 AM if you wish. Just write it in on your schedule. However, the first drop-in time does not begin until 8 AM,

⇒ During the days, SLC's are scheduled on the half hour (7:30, 8:30, etc), drop in's on the hour (8, 9, etc). Tuesday evening is an exception with the SLC's scheduled at 5, 6, and 7 and drop in's on the half hour.

⇒ There seems to be no "perfect" way to schedule for the evening. If the dinner break is scheduled later, then we end up staying later to have enough time slots for SLC's. Since what we did last year seemed to work as well as any, we'll stick to those times for dinner.

⇒ As a general rule, you may schedule up to three conferences at a time, four during the evening slots. Please do not schedule more than that unless it just can't be avoided.

⇒ You are responsible for scheduling your own breaks during slots reserved for student led conferencing.

⇒ You **must** be in your room during drop-in times.

⇒ Families will be scheduled through the office on Monday and Tuesday. When you get your schedules for Wednesday, you may have conferences already scheduled. Do not change a scheduled student without checking with student services first.

⇒ As we did last year, a conference on Student Led Conferencing will be held on Monday. We will be having participants visit rooms during the 9:30 and 10:30 slots (students will be asked if it's ok), so please try and schedule some "good" ones during those time slots. Thanks.

⇒ You are responsible for filling out a postcard for each of your students (even those scheduled through the office). This includes putting the label on the back.

⇒ Schedule all of your students, **even those that are absent**. Parents will be able to call the office to change their appointment if necessary.

⇒ At the end of your case manager time on Wednesday, return your Postcards and Schedules to student services.

⇒ Schedules will be kept in student services until just prior to the conferences so that Carol can make changes if a parent should call.

Countdown to Conferences!

By Wednesday the 10th each case manager will receive a packet containing the following:

- ✍ Folders to use for portfolios
- ✍ Student Procedure Sheets
- ✍ Table of Content Sheets
- ✍ Goals for Success Sheets
- ✍ Parent Homework Letter
- ✍ Reminder invitations for the conference

1. **Classroom Practice**

   Students should come to case manager on Monday the 15th having practiced sharing their work samples. For each piece, the student should be able to share:
   - ☆ What the assignment was
   - ☆ What knowledge or skills was learned by doing it
   - ☆ What process was used to complete the piece
   - ☆ A key portion of the self-reflection (highlighting it works well)

2. **Student Procedures for Conferencing**

   The student procedure sheet is to be used to help your students learn the process to follow during the student-led conference. Please be sure your students are familiar with the steps. It may be helpful for the students if they staple the sheet to the inside cover of the portfolio.

3. **Goal Setting**

   Ideas for goal setting – if your students have trouble thinking of their strengths and areas for growth, have them read through their self-reflections to get ideas. Have students be specific in setting their goals. "Math" is not a goal, "Turning in my math homework on time" is. Since the form is on NCR paper, you may wish to have them do a rough draft of their goals on another sheet of paper.

4. **Parent Homework**

   Have your students read over the form. Emphasize that nothing will happen to them if their parents choose not to write a letter. They should simply ask their parents to "do their homework." The letters from the parents can be kept at home or returned to school to be put in the portfolio.

5. **The role of the case manager during the conference**

   As a case manager, it is your responsibility to be present during the conferences but not necessarily a "part" of the conference. Students should introduce you to their parents/guardian at the beginning. Since you may have up to 4 happening simultaneously, monitor the conferences by careful listening and be ready to help out if you see a student is struggling. Touch base with the parents near the

(continued)

end of the conference. If at all possible, try to join each conference during the goal setting or to be sure the proper items are taken and left. It is fine to step outside your room for a few minutes to get something, but for the most part you should be visible. Please do not use the time for lengthy conversations with other teachers.

6. **What to keep and what to leave**
   All student work should be left in the portfolio as some of it may be used for CIM work. Parents may take home:
   - The report card
   - A copy of the Goal Sheet
   - The Parent Homework assignment

   There will be some other info to give out, (ie: parent newsletter, etc.). You will get copies of it by Monday morning the 23rd.

7. **Drop-in Time**
   <u>**You must be in your room and available during all drop-in times.**</u>

8. **Practicing**
   Monday – Organize the portfolio and fill out the table of contents.
   Tuesday -- Focus on the goal setting process
   Wednesday – A short video that models a SLC will be shown over the system
   Finish goal setting
   Thurs, Fri - Practice, practice, practice. Break students into groups of 2 or 3 to role play the conference. Changing groups daily helps eliminate the "boredom" factor. <u>Every student should have the opportunity to practice their entire conference 2 to 3 times.</u> Channel 1 will be shown on Friday, but you will need to turn on your set to see it.

9. **Reminder Invitations**
   Have your students fill these out on Friday the 19th and take home as a reminder to parents.

10. **Celebration**
    You will meet with your case manager group on Wednesday, Dec. 1 for a celebration – goodies will be provided. More info at a later date.

11. **"Unloading" the work**
    Thursday, Dec. 2 will be the day to return work to teachers. Students will report to 1st period for attendance. After the morning announcements, students will be dismissed to go to their case manager to pick up their portfolio and return immediately to class. During the day, they will return work to their teachers. Work left over at the end of the day may be taken home. PE and Electives Teachers – if you need work back from students, let them know to bring it to you.

Wrap-Up of Student Led Conferences

A big thank you to everyone for helping our conference process go smoothly. Based on the parent feedback forms, 63% strongly agreed and 34% agreed that student led conferences were valuable and informative!

Please attend to the following details so we can wrap up our conferences for this year.

☆ If you have a folder for a student that did not show up for the conference <u>and</u> you do not have a conference scheduled for that student, give the folder to Carol.

☆ An attempt will be made to reschedule the conference. If that is not possible, we will be inviting parent volunteers to come in and listen to conferences so that all students will have an opportunity to share. If you'd like to listen to a conference or two, let Carol know.

☆ Please complete the staff feedback form and turn it in by Thursday.

☆ On Wednesday, December 1 we will have Case Managers during e-lab. Orally debrief with your students on how they felt it went. We will provide ice creams bars as a treat for a job well done. Details to come.

☆ Case Managers should remove the yellow "Goals for Success" copy from the portfolios and place them in the student's CIM file. We will have a revisiting goals day in about 6 weeks or so.

☆ Thursday, December 2 will be used as "Unloading" Day -- Students will pick up their portfolio from their case manager in AM and return work through the day. Any work not needed in the future should be sent home with the student.

Self-Reflection — Writing

First, look over the writing you have done this trimester then thoughtfully answer the questions below. Think of yourself as a writer!

1. What does someone have to do in order to be a good writer?

2. What is the most important or useful thing you've learned as a writer?

3. What one thing in writing do you feel more confident about than you did at the beginning of the school year?

4. What could you teach someone about writing?

5. Which writing trait is your strongest? Why?

6. Which writing trait do you feel is your weakest?

7. Which mode of writing do you enjoy the most/ Why?

8. What still confuses you?

9. What can I (the teacher) do to help you be a better writer?

10. What kind of writing would you like to do in the future?

11. What are your writing goals for the next trimester?

Self-Reflection on an Individual Piece of Writing

Name_____

Title of piece_____   Date_____

Look at carefully at your personal narrative.   Answer the following questions thoughtfully.

1. What do you see as the special strengths of this paper?

2. What was especially important when you were writing this piece?

3. What have you learned about writing from your work on this piece?

4. What skills does this piece of writing show you possess?

5. What skills does this piece of writing show you need to develop further?

6. If you could go on with this piece, what would you do?

7. Additional comments you would like me to know about you and your writing:

Writing Summary – Fall 1999
Core: Munroe/Coleman

Name _____ Date _____

1. List the pieces of writing you completed this trimester:

    Topic/Title   Mode

    1._____   _____

    2._____   _____

    3._____   _____

2. What piece of writing do you consider your most effective?

3. Why? What did you do as an author? Cite examples if necessary.

4. What new skills do you need to work on as a writer? Who can help you with this skill?

    •
    •
    •
    •

5. What are your writing goals for the rest of the year? How will you accomplish them?

Self-Reflection = Reading

First look over your reading responses, your list of books you have read, and your reading work. As you answer these questions, think about how you have grown as a reader this trimester.

What has been the most rewarding to you in the way we have reading workshop in our classroom? How has it changed you as a reader?

What are your strengths as a reader?

What would you like to improve on as a reader?

What's the best book you've read this trimester?

What makes this one of the best for you?

What's the most significant thing you learned from this book and/or discovered about yourself as you read it?

What genres of books would you like to read in the future?

What can I (the teacher) help you do as a reader?

What goals do you plan for yourself as a reader?

Project Evaluation
The Alice in Wonderland ABC Booklet
October 1999 / Munroe-Coleman

Name_____

Whew!!! Your hard work and effort has paid off. You have completed this project to show your understanding of the elements of literature, the literary devices, and the content of the novel, *Alice in Wonderland.* Quite an undertaking, but you are done. Now, please respond thoughtfully to the following questions.

1. Describe the process you went through to complete the booklet. (Think back to mini-lessons on games/riddles, devices, reading aloud, discussions, finding quotes for your pages, designing each page, writing and illustrating the booklet, editing, and the people who helped you.)

2. What were your strengths for this project? *Examples:* creative ideas, comprehension of the novel, personal examples, self-directed learning, time management, understanding of the elements-devices, lay-out and design, citations.
   -
   -
   -
   -
   -

3.   Problems encountered   Solutions to problems

4. Rate your understanding of the elements of literature and literary devices on a scale of 1 - 10.

Not at 0 $\longleftarrow$ ———————————————— $\longrightarrow$ 10 **I get**
  all!   5   **it!**

5. When you look at your ABC book, what thoughts go through your mind?

6. Other comments that would be helpful for me to know that I cannot tell from your finished booklet...

Sample I-Search Introduction/Self-Reflection
Ancient Egypt
3100 B.C. - 30 B.C.
Mrs. Sessions - Core

(Think of your own catchy beginning/lead! Here's mine…)

As you read through my exploration of _____, sit back, relax, and take a trip back into the times of pharaohs, pyramids, and ancient mysteries. I chose the topic of _____ because _____

_____

I started my research on (month, day, year) and completed it on (month, day, year). The only information I knew about before I began my in-depth study was

_____

I began my research by _____.

I found it easy to _____, but I

got frustrated when _____

Some interesting information I learned was _____

_____

One thing I found that surprised me was _____

_____

The project I made was _____. It enhanced my study of

_____ by _____

If I did this research and project again I would _____

_____

**(End with a conclusion that is catchy and fun and makes the reader want to
read your thoughts and information about your topic.)**

Oral Presentation Self-Reflection

Name:_____   Topic: _____

Date:_____

Directions: Take a few minutes to think back over your presentation and then answer the following questions.

1. Looking back over your presentation, what were your thoughts and reactions about how you did?

2. What do you think were the strengths of your presentation? (Refer to the scoring guide to be specific)

3. If you could redo your presentation, what would you like to do differently?

4. What visual aid(s) and/or enhancers did you use in this speech?

How were they effective? (Size, clarity, ease of use, referring to them during the presentation, etc.)

5. What are some goals (or areas to improve) you'd like to see yourself accomplish for your next speech?

Portfolio Cover Letter

Complete the following paragraphs and staple your letter to your best, worst, and most challenging papers. Make sure to label your papers "best," "worst," and "most challenging." Remember this is your letter. You may change or add paragraphs or whatever. Use this as a general outline.

Dear

       Mathematical topics we've studied are...

       I learned that...

       I chose _____ as my "best" work for the following three reasons:

       I chose _____ as my "worst" work for the following three reasons:

       I chose _____ as my "most challenging" work for the following three reasons:

       I feel I progressed in...

       I feel I need to work on...

                               Sincerely,

SELF-REFLECTION... ROCKETRY SCIENCE UNIT

Describe the 3 LAB experiments we have completed in Science Class Rocketry Unit. Tell me what you have learned.

List some Rocket LAB Variables that may have altered the final outcomes of launch angle and volume tests.

1.
2.
3.
4.
5.
6.

Have you enjoyed this activity sofar? Why? Please explain.

Several scientific principles were explored in the Diving Tube Lab. List them. (How does this lab apply to life outside the Science classroom)

I struggled with.....

I really enjoyed.....

NAME _____ P₁ - MCNICHOL

Name _____   Period _____

Decision Tree Reflection and Self-Evaluation

My situation was:

The choices I had were:

The choice I made was:

I chose it because:

The part of this assignment I found to be easiest was:

The part that was hardest was:

...because:

...because:

If I did this project again, I would:

NAME: _____

GRADE: _____

PERIOD: _____

Self-Reflection for Physical Education

1)   My strengths in Physical Education are: _____

_____

_____

_____

_____

_____

2)   What could I do to improve in Physical Education and how? (behavior, participation, effort, honesty, sportsmanship)

_____

_____

_____

_____

_____

_____

3)   I can improve my personal fitness level during Physical Education class by:

_____

_____

_____

_____

_____

_____

4)   I can further enhance my personal fitness by:_____

_____

_____

_____